THE
HANSA

THE
HANSA

by
E. Gee Nash

BARNES
&NOBLE
BOOKS
NEW YORK

Originally published in 1929.

This edition published by Barnes & Noble, Inc.

1995 Barnes & Noble Books

ISBN 1-56619-867-4

Printed and bound in the United States of America

M 9 8 7 6 5 4 3 2 1

CONTENTS

Part III

DECLINE OF THE HANSEATIC LEAGUE

PART I

RISE OF THE HANSEATIC LEAGUE

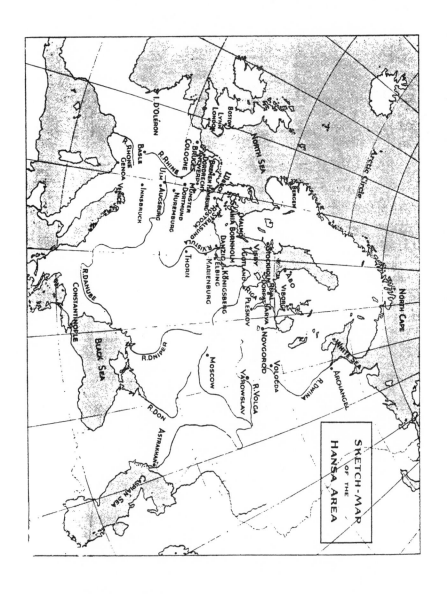

SKETCH-MAP
OF THE
HANSA AREA

CHAPTER I

A T first sight it would appear that the Hanseatic
League sprang into being as a perfected
organization in the thirteenth century. Its first records
show it as a body in good working order, with an
immense amount of power, well-thought-out and
stringently enforced laws ; but of course this is quite
impossible, so we can only infer that its earliest activities were veiled in mystery, and that, in the beginning,
it kept no records of its doings.

This is easily understandable ; for, in the turbulent
time in which the League arose, it must have been
extremely unpopular with the ruling powers and so
probably dared not keep any written records.

The name " Hansa " as applied to the League has
an obscure origin. The word is to be found in Gothic,
where it is generally applied to a company of com-
batant men ; then, later on, it was used as the title
of a tax on trade goods. Perhaps the heads of the
League, not lacking in a sense of humour, decided on
that name for an organization which would most
certainly benefit largely by taxes on merchandise, and
would, in all probability, be compelled to band themselves into companies of combatants to protect their

1

interests. Whatever decided them on that choice of a name it was never applied to the League until after its first war, the successful war with Valdemar Atterdag, of Denmark, when the League used it in the Treaty of Stralsund, 1370—that amazing document which first proclaimed the Hanseatic League as a power to be reckoned with.

All early records point to the organization having been originally formed as a " merchant league," without any idea of " civic " status.

" In England, the first records mention ' Hansa domus *mercatorum* Alemannie.'

" In Norway, about 1343, ' *Mercatores* de Hansa Theutonicorum.'

" In Novgorod, in 1350, ' Theutonicorum Hansa *mercatories*.' " [1]

To appreciate the conditions which led to the foundation of such an organization, it is essential to have some slight idea of the state of Central Europe in the days of Feudalism and under the rule of the Holy Roman Empire ; for it was at that time, when conditions were so terrible for the people, that, without some protection, trade could never have been established, let alone have grown and expanded, that the leagues of cities gradually came into being.

Undoubtedly the first foundation-stones of the cities as civic bodies were laid in very early days ; and, to understand the rapid growth of German trade, one must realize that feudalism in Central Europe never gained the utter subjection of the people as it did in England,

[1] *Zur Entstehung und Bedeutung der deutschen Hanse,* Dr. Walther Stein.

a fact that led to the development of the merchant spirit
in Germans long before that spirit quickened to life
in the English people.

In these times of peace and prosperity, it is almost
impossible to realize the state of Europe during the
tenth, eleventh and twelfth centuries. Gone was the
might of the Roman Empire, and with it all the trading
and travelling facilities it had established, shattered by
the invading hordes of barbarians. Then came the
evil days of Feudalism, and the Holy Roman Empire,
under whose rule the land was subdivided into
provinces governed by Margraves, Dukes and Barons,
each constantly warring with his neighbour, and barter-
ing, mortgaging and giving away portions of his lands,
till in the ensuing confusion, there was little or no
security for those members of the community who
were struggling to establish some stable form of trade.

But it is an ill wind that blows no one any good,
for, while the ruling classes fought one another, the
slowly growing burgher classes took advantage of their
constant need for money and gained privilege after
privilege.

The first merchants were men (not necessarily Jews,
although one is apt to assume that a travelling pedlar
in Europe is, and was, always a Jew) who wandered
round the country with their packs on their backs ;
or, if they were in slightly better circumstances, on
horses or mules ; later to expand into a caravan of
baggage carts, with perhaps a small body of paid
soldiers to protect them from the robbers who infested
the lonely tracts of country.

It is not usual to associate any very great amount

of physical courage with the merchant classes, but
these men undoubtedly took their lives in their hands
at every hour of the day. This did not stop their
enterprise ; the lust for buying and selling was strong
in their blood, and, under the most fearful conditions
of hardship and danger, they went their weary way
over the ill-conditioned roads to convey their merchandise from place to place, braving the dangers of pillage
and death at the hands of the various Barons and
powerful dignitaries of the Church—for their holy
calling did not make the latter any the less eager for
temporal riches.

Starting with a rude collection of huts, built round
a Baron's castle or a rich monastery, raised and brought
together by the various craftsmen with the sole intention of supplying their ruler with the goods he
required, these villages grew till they produced more
than the castle could use, and so they started exchanging
and selling goods in the country round about. Very
gradually they became rich enough to lend money to
their Barons, who were in constant need of it for their
interminable internal wars ; and in return for this
money the merchants did not ask for interest but,
instead, they begged certain privileges : at first merely
the rights of fishing and hunting, then the right of
bearing arms, then the privilege of holding City
Councils, and finally they demanded a City Charter
by which they might manage their own affairs without
the interference of their over-lord. It was this City
Charter which gradually led up to the administration
of Civil Laws. Now the Baron, a man more skilled
in war than in foresight, preferred to grant their requests

rather than to go to the Jews, the recognized money-lenders, who, even at an early date, carried on a flourishing business in usury, and to whom they would have had to pay anything from forty to sixty per cent. interest. It never entered their heads that the granting of these minor privileges was to be the first stepping-stone to a power which would eventually wipe them off the face of Europe. But great things often have such small and insignificant beginnings, and these privileges were indeed the foundation-stones of the City Charters, and the far-reaching Civic power that grew and grew till it was mighty enough to dictate to Kings and Emperors.

A great impetus was given to trading by the Crusades, as the Barons required a great deal of ready money, for they could not carry great stores of food and necessaries with them on their journeys. The Crusades also did a great deal towards reviving art and culture, for they opened up new countries, and many a man returned with fresh ideas for the betterment of conditions.

With Europe in the state it was in at that time—with hardly any roads, and the ones there were almost always foot deep in mud—the travelling merchants had a hazardous time, and their difficulties were added to by the lawless state of the whole country.

Not only was it infested with robber bands, but every castle was a menace to travellers. The Barons, and the heads of the Church as well, levied tolls on all the roads that ran through their provinces, and, by the most stringent laws, no merchant was allowed to travel by any but a toll road ; if he were seized on a by-road his goods, and often his life, were forfeit.

So, travelling on the toll roads, the merchant had to pay constant dues, and even then his life was in danger if the Baron happened to think he would like the whole load of merchandise, and not only his heavy percentage.

Then, when he had reached another trading centre and had so far escaped with his life and a portion of his goods intact, the poor man's troubles were by no means at an end. In all probability the city lay in another province under totally different jurisdiction, and so he, as a stranger, with no claim to justice, was open to the attacks of any ill-intentioned persons.

So much for the dangers of land travel ! The daring merchant who got together goods and men for a sea venture was in little better state.

At that time there were no known laws of navigation, and the boats, in the earliest instance rowed by banks of oars, were obliged to creep round the shores, seldom if ever daring to go out of sight of land. Thus they were an easy prey for the many bands of pirates who infested the shores of the Baltic Sea, for it was mainly round the Baltic that the first German merchants made their voyages.

Nor were pirates their only menace, for according to the ancient law of " Strandgut " all merchandise washed up on to the shore belonged, in its entirety, to the owner of that land, and many a landowner was an expert at the gentle art of wrecking and did a flourishing trade in merchandise obtained in this way.

Undoubtedly it was the prevailing conditions of danger that made the merchants realize that they must try and obtain some privileges and protection and that any organization to this end must originate with themselves, and not be dependent upon the fluctuations of the ruling powers. It was the first attempt at attaining this protection that led to the foundation of the Swabian, Wendish and Baltic Leagues of Cities, at first established for the mutual protection of German merchants throughout Germany, then expanding into the far-reaching Hanseatic organization.

The need for such a protective league will be more easily understood when one realizes that, as late as the latter part of the last century, it was necessary for English merchants abroad to protect their interests by founding a counterpart of the Hanseatic League in the present-day Chambers of Commerce ; such as the British Chamber of Commerce in Paris, founded in 1873, which was established by British merchants resident in Paris for the protection of their trade interests ; and afterwards admitted firms trading with, but not resident in, Paris and now represents general British trade interests in French markets.

But as I have said, the origin of the League is veiled in mystery. It arose so gradually, and there are so many gaps in its history before 1241 that it is almost impossible to piece together a coherent story of its activities. For instance, as far back as the tenth century there are records of the German merchants having been granted equal privileges with the English merchants. The toll for this privilege they paid in kind, twice a year, and it consisted of " Two lengths of cloth, six pairs of gloves (a very usual payment in those times), two ankers of vinegar, and about twelve pounds of pepper "—then a great rarity, and afterwards a German monopoly (vide the News Letters of the Counts Fugger of Augsburg).

The first cities to join themselves into a Protective League were the Rhine towns, and they did not accomplish it without a great deal of opposition from the ruling classes ; but by this time the towns were in a position to insist on their rights, and the League flourished.

It was only natural that the Rhine should produce a series of important towns, as that river was the waterway for the carrying trade for the goods imported from the East via Italy.

The example of the Rhine towns was quickly followed by the federation of Baltic Cities which, having started as a separate organization, was finally developed into the Hanseatic League.

During the reign of Frederick Barbarossa, the " city state " made great strides, and the merchant leagues gained many privileges both at home and abroad. In 1157 the Emperor made a treaty with Henry II concerning the privileges of merchants in their respective countries. This treaty, certainly the first of any importance bearing on the guild of German merchants which later on was to be known as the Hanseatic League, ran as follows :

" The league betweene Henry the second and Fredericke Barbarossa, Emperour of Germanie, wherein is mention of friendly traffike betweene the Marchants of the Empire and England, confirmed in the yeere of our Lord 1157, recorded in the first Booke and seventeenth Chapter of Radevicus Canonicus Frisingensis, being an appendix to Otto Frisingensis.

" There were present also at the same time, the messengers of Henry, King of England, presenting divers rich and precious gifts, and that with great learning and eloquence of speech. Amongst the which we saw a pavilion, most large in quantity, and most excellent in quality. For if you desire to know the quantitie thereof, it could not be erected without engines and a kinde of instruments, and maine force : if the qualitie, I thinke there was never any furniture of the same kinde, that surpassed the same either in stuffe or workemanship. The said King directed his letters also, full of sugred speeches, the tenour whereof was this that followeth.

" To his entirely beloved friend Frederick, by the Grace of God, Emperour of the Romans, most invincible, Henry, King of England, Duke of Normandie and Aquitaine, Earle of Anjou, wisheth health and concorde of sincere amitie. We doe render unto your highnes (most renowmed and peerelesse Prince) exceeding great thanks for that you have so graciously vouchsafed by your messengers to visite us, in your letters to salute us, with your gifts to prevent us, and (which wee doe more highly esteeme of then all the rest) to beginne a league of peace and friendship betweene us. We rejoyced, and in a maner sensibily felt ourselves to bee greatly emboldened, and our courage to increase, whilest your promise whereby you put us in good comfort, did make us more cheereful and resolute, in managing the affaires of our kingdome.

" We rejoyced (I say) and in our secret cogitations did humble obeisance unto your Majestie, giving you at this time to understand from the sincere and unfained affection of our heart, that whatsoever we shal know to tend unto your honour, we are, to our power most ready to put in practise. Our Kingdome, and whatsoever is under our jurisdiction we doe offer unto you, and commit the same unto your highnesse, that all matters may be disposed according to your direction, and that your pleasure may in all things be fulfilled. Let there be therefore betweene ourselves and our subjects, an indivisible unitie of friendship and peace, and safe trade of marchandize : yet so, as that unto you (who excell in dignitie) authoritie in commanding may bee ascribed, and diligence in obeying shall not want in us. And as the liberalitie of your rewards doeth often put us in rememberence of your Majestie, even so in like maner sending unto your Highnesse the most rare things in our custodie, and which we thought should be most acceptable unto you, wee doe most heartily wish that yourselfe also would not altogether bee unmindefull of us. Have respect therefore not unto the gifts, but unto the affection of the giver, and accept of them with that minde, wherewith they are offered unto you." [1]

Thus by 1157 the cities had attained a position in which they were able to enter into negotiations with the Emperor demanding that he should make treaties for them, so that they could obtain protection in foreign cities outside his Empire. The need for this protection was occasioned in no small degree by the difficulties of navigation. Merchants who undertook sea voyages had to be prepared to sojourn for many months in strange lands. They had to stop there until their goods were sold, and then it was very possibly too late in the year for them to set out for home. In those days, with navigation and ships in their infancy (though they were making strides forward every year), the ships dare not put to sea during the winter months ; therefore certain sea laws were drawn up, under one of which no ships

[1] *The English Voyages*, Hakluyt, Vol. I, p. 107. (Everyman Edition.)

were supposed to sail between the dates of November 11th and February 2nd ; this law was relaxed in the cases of ships carrying certain commodities, namely those which were required for the great fasts and feasts of the Church, which merchandise was termed " valued." A considerable part of the League's sea activities was with the various trading centres round the Baltic shores, and the Baltic in winter is a sea that even to-day, with our marvellous ships and our exact science of navigation, can present difficult problems to winter travel, so what must it have been in those days when tiny ships crept round the shores from place to place, afraid of going out to sea lest they lost their bearings, and even more afraid of hugging the shores lest they were fallen upon by the bold and daring pirates of the Baltic ?

One must remember that the development of civilization in Eastern and Central Europe was very greatly retarded, and that it was long before any of the German cities could compare with those of the Mediterranean.

Italy never suffered after the fall of Rome as did the other parts of Europe ; and it kept, to a large extent, its civilization, art and culture, and above all its thriving trade. In fact, the Italian cities were instrumental in moulding the progress of the German cities, for, as conditions got better and merchants travelled more and more widely over the old trade routes, they brought back with them from Italy many of the ideas of art, culture and progress, finally to incorporate them in their own cities.

It is strange to think that the English, who have always been the sea-going nation *par excellence*, should have lagged so far behind in the matter of trade ; but this was due in no small degree to the favour that was shown to foreign merchants by the ruling powers in England up to the reign of Elizabeth. This was always far greater than that shown to the earliest English merchants abroad ; in fact, the English merchants required to have their wits sharpened by the constant friction with the Hanseats before they awoke to the realization of the enormous wealth they had in their midst. Once that awakening began it was not long before England took her proper place in the trading world, but before that day dawned the Germans had been skimming the cream off European trade for several centuries.

Thus began the guilds of cities, first established with the idea of protecting the merchants within Germany, then growing and expanding till their protection covered men trading in foreign lands. The treaty between Barbarossa of Germany and Henry II of England marks the first real expansion of the League, and from that date onwards it was to grow year by year till, with the Treaty of Stralsund in 1370, the Hanseatic League was recognized as one of the greatest powers in Europe.

From that date one can trace the League as an established body with written records, many of which exist to this day and may be consulted in the various city archives throughout Germany and Scandinavia.

The League is easily traceable through three phases, its growth, apogee and decline, and it has to be followed in several countries : Germany (possessing by far the greatest number of Hansa towns), Russia, Scandinavia, the Netherlands and England, with a slightly different organization trading under the Hansa in Italy.

One by one the cities rose to fame and power, lived their great day and declined till their places were taken by new towns.

With grim tenacity and determination the League held its various Kontors in far-flung outposts of Europe, suffering many hardships, often expelled, yet ever returning, tempted by the glittering promise of riches.

The whole history of the Hanseatic League, together with that of our own Merchant Venturers, is so full of courage and the spirit of adventure that it must completely alter our ideas of the merchant classes. These were no men cringing behind their counters, armed solely with a yard-stick, but stout fellows who took their lives in their hands, voyaged in wretched boats across uncharted seas, sold their goods in hostile towns in foreign countries, and lived for months at a time among people who seldom bore them any goodwill.

Yet they never drew back : they were traders born, and no amount of danger stopped them. So, from the small dealings of the first pedlar carrying his pack upon his aching back, to the great merchant princes like the Counts Fugger of Augsburg, trade went ever forward, and through these intrepid merchants the might and power of the cities grew and grew till the great trading league known as the Hanseatic League was stronger than Kings and Emperors. It ruled its subject cities with a hand of iron, and developed the whole wonderful system of civic laws that gave peace and freedom to the countries.

This mighty League, whose foundations were raised on the courage and endurance of the merchants whom history has always looked down upon, and compared unfavourably with the fighting classes, was a power for good in the land. Who was the greater, the merchant who suffered and helped to build a lasting civic organization, or the soldiers who ravaged Europe, leaving behind them nothing but waste and pillaged tracts ?

All through the ages little honour has been done to the merchant classes, yet the history of trade is the history of fruitful endeavour, and many a patient, heroic man lost his life in those early trading ventures, crossing bitter seas in search of new markets. All unknown they suffered and perished and theirs is not the least among the world's unsung Odysseys.

KEYS

CHAPTER II

NATURALLY the cities affiliated to the Hanseatic
League had grown up in the vicinity of good
water-ways, trade routes, and round the mouths of
rivers opening into the various seas. The German
cities were more closely gathered round the rivers Oder,
Elbe, Weser, Ems and Rhine ; and the Flanders cities on
the Rhine and Maas. A question frequently asked is,
" Which were the Hanseatic Cities ? " but this cannot
be answered definitely, for towns were always joining
and leaving, so that there was a constant fluctuation
in the number of cities under the League. None of the
authorities' lists agree. Sartorius, the great early writer
on the Hansa, gives a long list, but even he leaves out
some important towns, besides utterly ignoring all
those outside Germany !

However, it is quite safe to say that all the important
towns in Germany, and most of the important ones in
the Low Countries and England, belonged, at one time
or another, to the Hanseatic League during the thirteenth, fourteenth and fifteenth centuries.

The most important and lasting members were, of
course, Lübeck, Bremen and Hamburg, which persisted
from the beginning to the end of the Hanseatic League.

The other leading towns and cities were, at different periods, Bergen, Novgorod, Danzig, Visby, Reval, Riga, Stralsund, Zoest, Dortmund, Königsberg, Elbing, Thorn, Rostock, Brunswick, Münster, Tangermunde, Trävemunde, Wismar, Stargard, Friburg, Frankfurt, Cologne, Hamlin, Magdeburg; in Flanders—Ghent, Bruges, Antwerp, Dordrecht; and in England, London, King's Lynn. The south German cities of Augsburg, Ulm and Nuremberg, which were in direct communication with Venice, where the Hansa held a modified Kontor, were never so closely connected with the Hansa organization, although they were affiliated to it.

Of course there were some cities in France, the Netherlands, Spain, Portugal and England with which the Hansa had dealings, but which never actually came under the heading of Hanseatic Cities.

Some of the most important trading-posts of the League were founded in places which scarcely merited the name of cities. Novgorod was an outpost in the very wilds of Russia and Bergen, in the earliest days of the Hansa, had little claim to civic distinction, but that did not prevent their being flourishing trading centres.

After the founding of the German League of Cities, the heads of the Hansa turned their eyes towards the very flourishing trade round the Baltic coasts.

This trade was the herring fishery, for at that time the herring spawned in the Baltic off the Pomeranian coast and the islands of Rügen, Bornholm and Gotland.

The great importance of this industry was due to the enormous amount of fish eaten throughout Europe on the many fast days of the Roman Catholic and Greek Orthodox Churches.

At that time there were no facilities for carrying the fish far inland quickly enough to keep it fresh, so, with the aid of the salt deposits round the Baltic, the Danes had invented an excellent method of salting the fish. Thus cured it could be sent far inland and still arrive in an eatable, if extremely unpalatable, condition. This industry had brought much wealth to the Baltic cities, and at a very early date the Hanseats at Lübeck realized the need for establishing close connections with these towns, especially with that of Visby, on the island of Gotland.

So the most important commodity that was carried by the early Hanseats was salt herring. In fact, herrings played such an important part in mediæval trade that the changes in their spawning grounds led to the rise and fall of whole cities, even of nations.

Their migration in the early fifteenth century to the coasts of the North Sea led to the rise of the Netherlands, and the ruin of many of the Baltic towns.

It was for the ships carrying this important cargo for the great Lenten fasts that the laws for ship sailing were relaxed. In fact, a cargo of herring, cod and beer was esteemed a " cargo precious in value."

But, having procured fleets for the herring carrying trade, the Hansa had no intention of allowing them to remain idle for the rest of the year, so they used them as general cargo boats. Having discharged their fish, they brought back cargoes of other goods. One is apt to think of the merchandise of the twelfth and thirteenth centuries as probably poor and uninteresting, but the records of the Hansa cargoes show that it was anything but that. Their trade was rich and varied ; and, if

the times were rude and violent in appetite and amusement, they lacked few of the creature comforts, and
even provided the rich with not a little luxury.

The Hansa were the first to recognize the enormous
value of the natural resources of Russia, then in a state
of barbarism, and they were not slow in establishing
themselves at Novgorod.

Novgorod, lying as it did on the direct trade route
from the Black Sea and the Bosphorus to the Baltic,
and near the junction of four great water-ways,
provided the Hansa with Oriental merchandise as well
as with all the varied products of the country itself.

Russia had vast natural resources and, moreover,
ones that were at that time especially valuable. The
great forests provided timber, tar and pitch, and a large
quantity of honey and wax, the latter being commodities
of extreme value, as honey was then the only known
means of sweetening food and wax was used for the
many candles needed for the elaborate rituals of the
Roman Catholic and Greek Orthodox Churches.

Wax was one of the most expensive products of those
times, often costing as much as £3 or £4 a pound. It
figures largely in royal presentations—Edward III receiving one hundred pounds of wax, among other gifts,
from the City of London.

Then Russia teemed with fur-bearing animals and
their skins were a great source of profit to the Hanseatic
League. The merchants paid very little for the
roughly cured skins and after having worked them—
for there were excellent furriers in those times—they
sold them, at enormous profit, for the universal fur
trimmings to the heavy, sumptuous robes that were

the everyday dress of the burgher and merchant classes.

Nor were these the only products of Russia, for there was a lively trade in skins and tallow.

The finding of so many Eastern coins in Visby and Northern Europe points clearly to the fact that the Oriental traders penetrated at least as far as Novgorod, and there is evidence that they drove a brisk trade in furs.

From Italy the Hansa brought all the luxurious products of Eastern trade : embroidery, stamped leather work, silks, velvets, heavily chased metal, gold, silver and precious gems ; also cargoes of fruits and spices.

To these countries they sent in return the excellent Flemish cloth and linen, and the rougher English and German weaves ; salt fish and the heavy, intoxicating beer brewed in North Germany, the beer for which Hamburg was so justly famous, and which was the general drink of the lower classes of the period and therefore a very valuable monopoly.

Nor did they overlook the garish tastes of the semi-barbarous Russian princelings—for them they carried all the brilliant Oriental merchandise.

From Sweden they fetched copper and iron ; Storakopparberget, the most famous copper mine in Europe, dates back from a very early age, its first charter, with five great, hanging seals, is dated 1288, and there is much evidence that the Germans—especially the Lübeckers—had a very close connection with this mine and its working.

Storakopparberget also produced a certain amount of silver, and legend has it that a certain Lübeck merchant loaded a ship with a cargo of silver and sailed away home to Lübeck with his prize.

From the Swedish province of Blekinge, the Hansa brought granite—very largely used in the church architecture of the day—and from the islands of Bornholm and Gotland they obtained limestone for civic buildings.

Much grain was exported from Prussia and the Baltic provinces. An interesting proof of this fact is that in 1390 an enterprising Lord Mayor of London, Adam Bamme, goldsmith, imported corn from there with which to relieve a famine in London, while in 1438, another Lord Mayor, Stephen Brown, grocer, imported corn from Prussia to such an extent that the price of wheat was reduced from 3s. a bushel to about 1s. 6d. By the Charter of 1282, granting the Hansa merchants the enjoyment of all their ancient liberties in London, they were permitted to sell grain for forty days after its arrival. This importation of foreign grain so incensed the English merchants that in 1463 an Act of Parliament was passed suspending the importation of grain till its price had passed a certain figure.[1]

Another factor which was instrumental in the development of trade, especially throughout the Prussian provinces, was the organization known as the Order of Teutonic Knights. After 1309, when the headquarters of the Teutonic Knights was transferred from Venice to Marienburg, on the Vistula, the Order began to take a prominent part, together with the Hanseatic League, in the *Drangnachusten* of the twelfth, thirteenth and fourteenth centuries.

[1] Authority : Emile Worms, *Histoire Commerciale de la Ligue Hanséatique*. Paris, 1864.

Even at this early date, the original intention of the Order—that of succouring the poor and sick and spreading Christianity—was rapidly vanishing in their intense zeal for spiritual and political power ; and few institutions, unless it was the Hansa, could compare in pomp and splendour with the Court of the Knights Teutonic at Marienburg. The Order had been responsible for the colonization of Prussia and their rule had resulted in such flourishing cities as Thorn, Elbing, Königsberg and Danzig, in all of which, while leaving them in a great degree free to rule themselves and levying no taxes, they levied custom dues.

Under Hartzman von Salza, the powerful and autocratic Grand Master, the Order entered into an alliance with the Hansa for the development of the German trade with Danzig and Thorn and up the water-ways of the Vistula. In fact, all the cities under the domination of the Teutonic Knights were at one time or another in the Hanseatic League.

Thorn, situated on the Vistula near the border of Poland, was the meeting-point of many trade routes from Poland, Prussia, Bohemia and Hungary, and as such it was the centre of a wide-flung trade. In 1403 the Grand Master of the Teutonic Knights, together with the heads of the Hanseatic League, resolved that no foreign merchants visiting the country should go anywhere except via Thorn. The following interesting documents testifying to the varied trade between Danzig and Thorn are still preserved in Hanseatic archives :

" Business association between Cueneze-Schwabe, called Le Vieux, of Danzig, and Cueneze-Sicz, of Thorn.

" The former sent English cloth which his brother
in his turn purveyed to the foreign merchants such as
Bartke-Snyder of Lemberg, Stadler d'Ofen, femme
Neuser of Breslau, Collitz of Prague, Frantzke d'Oels,
Pierre Graser of Cracow, etc.   In return Cueneze-Sicz
sent silver, furs and spices.

" In 1441 Pierre Huiszberg, of Cracow, entered
into an association with Einwald Wrige, of Danzig, to
pass between them an certain quantity of wood suitable for bows, in return for a cargo of cloth, wine,
salt and alum, that his agent Pierre Kreczemer, had
acquired in Flanders [1] and consigned to him (Wrige)
at Danzig." [2]

These two documents are of quite special interest,
for in the first one the mention of " femme " Neuser
plainly points to the fact that women played an active
part in commerce, and were held in sufficient repute
to be recognized and accredited agents.   The second
touches the hearts of all Englishmen, for it proves that
" The wood was grown in England, in England " is
rather more romantic than accurate.   An enormous
number of bow staves were exported through Danzig,
the wood coming from the vast Carpathian forests.   In
various records, mention is made of consignments of
" Wood for bow staves and for shippes," and so we lose
another illusion, for, to a certain extent, " our wooden
walls " and " our bows of Agincourt and Crecy " would
seem to have been " made in Germany " !

Danzig also did a large export trade in iron, lead and

---

[1] This cargo would probably be collected at Bruges, the Kontor
to which goods from the Steelyard in London were consigned.
(Author's note.)

[2] Emile Worms, *Histoire Commerciale de la Ligue Hanséatique.*
Paris, 1864.

copper from the mines of Hungary and Bohemia, and in coarse linen and grain from Poland.

In return, Danzig received Oriental merchandise down the trade routes from Novgorod, and did a thriving business in salt fish and bay salt from Visby. In fact, so well was the trade of Danzig developed under the Teutonic Knights that, after the fall of Thorn in the second half of the fifteenth century, Danzig automatically became the centre of the flourishing and widespread Vistula trade.

The following are a few extracts from the Customs Accounts of the Port of Southampton in 1300, showing the manner of entry (in Anglo-French) and the tolls paid on the various merchandise :

	£	s.	d.
" Of every hundred of boards for ships .			4
De chescun cent de Bordes p(ur) Nef			
Of a hundred of boards from Eastland [1] .			4
Del cent des Bordes de Estlond			
Of a hundred of stickes for long bows and cross-bows			2
Del cent des bastons p(ur) Arks et [p(ur) Arblastes			
Of a hundred of Sable, martin, Pole-cat, fox or cat skins			2
Of a bale of pepper, ginger, zedoury (valerian), cinnamon, galingale, mace, cubeb, cloves, saffron, grain (graine-greyn-dye in general, or 'kermes or scarlet' grain . . . editor's note) brazil	£1 (or value)		
Of a thousand of tin			10

[1] Eastland—Land of the Easterlings, i.e. round the Baltic. (Author's note.)

	£	s.	d.
or of a hundred			1
Of a thousand of copper . . .			10
or of a hundred			1
Of a hundred of brass			1
Of a fotmel [1] of lead			1/4
Of a fother of lead			6
Of a hundred of iron			1/4
and on the export of the same a halfpenny			
Of a ton of woad			1
Of a load of garlic (120 bunches—six pence)			12
Of a barrel of sturgeon " [2] . .			4

Hakluyt in his voyages gives the following amusing, and yet accurate account of the varied merchandise of the Hanseatic days :

OF THE COMMODITIES OF PRUSE, AND HIGH DUTCHMEN AND EASTERLINGS

Nowe Beere and Bakon bene fro Pruse ybrought
Into Flanders, as loved and farre ysought ;
Osmond, Copper, Bow-staves, Steele, and Wexe,
Peltreware and grey Pitch, Terre, Board, and Flexe :
And Colleyne threed, Fustian and Canvas,
Card, Bukeram : of olde time thus it was.
But the Flemmings among these things dere,
In common loven best Bakon and Beere.
Also Pruse men maken her adventure
Of Plate of silver of wedges good and sure
In great plentie which they bring and bye,
Out of the lands of Beame and Hungarie :
Which is increase full great unto their land,
And they bene laden, I understand,

[1] Fotmel = about 70 lbs. (Editor's note.)
[2] *The Oak Book of Southampton*, ed. P. Studer, pp. 5, 7, 9, 11.

With wollen cloth all maner of colours
By dyers crafted full divers, that ben ours.
And they adventure full greatly unto the Bay,
For salt that is needfull withouten nay.
Thus if they would not our friends bee,
We might lightly stoppe hem in the see ;
They should not passe our streemes withouten leve,
It would not be, but if we should hem greve.

OF THE COMMODITIES OF SPAINE AND OF FLANDERS

Knowe well all men that profits in certaine
Commodities called comming out of Spaine
And Marchandie, who so will weete what it is,
Bene Figs, Raisins, wine Bastard, and Datis,
And Licoris, Sivill oyle, and graine,
White Pastill Sope, and Waxe is not vayne.
Yron, Wooll, Wadmolle, Gotefell, Kidfell also :
For Poynt-makers full needefull bene they tweyn :
Saffron, Quicksilver, which owne Spaine Marchandy,
Is into Flanders shipped full craftily,
Unto Bruges as to her staple fayre ;
The Haven of Scluse hir Haven for her repayre
Which is cleped Swyn tho shippes giding ;
Where many vessels and fayre are abiding.
But these Marchandes with their shippes great,
And such chaffare as they bye and get
By the wayes must nede take on hand
By the coasts to passe of our England,
Betwixt Dover and Calais, this is no doubt,
Who can well els such matter bring about ?

And when these sayd Marchants discharged bee
Of Marchandie in Flanders nere the see,
Then they bee charged againe with Marchandy,
That to Flanders bougeth full richly.
Fine cloth of Ypre that named is better than ours,
Cloth of Curtrike, fine cloth of all colours,

Much Fustian, and also Linen cloth.
But Flemings, if yee bee not wroth,
The great substance of your cloth at the full
Yee wot ye make it of our English woll.

Then may it not sinke in mannis brayne,
But that it must this Marchandy of Spaine
Both out and in by our costes passe ;
Hee that sayd nay in witte was like an asse.
We should have peace with the grounds tweyne
Thus if this see were kept, I dare well sayne.
For Spaine and Flanders is as eche other brother,
And neither may well live without other ;
They may not liven to maintaine their degrees,
Without our English commodities :
Wolle and Tynne : for the woolle of England
Susteineth the Commons Flemmings I understand.
Then if England would her wolle restraine
From Flanders, this followeth in certaine,
Flanders of nede must with us have peace,
Or els she is destroyed without lees.
Also if Flanders thus destroyed bee :
Some Marchandie of Spaine will never ythee :
For destroyed it is, and as in cheeffe
The wolle of Spaine it commeth not to preeffe,
But if it be costed and menged well
Amongst the English wolle the greater delle,
For Spanish wooll in Flanders draped is,
And ever hath bee, that men have mind of this :
And yet wooll is one of the chiefe Marchandy
That longeth to Spaine : who so will espie,
It is of little value, trust unto mee,
With English wooll but if it menged bee.
Thus if the see be kept, than herken hether,
If these two lands comen not together :
So that the fleete of Flanders passe nought
That in the narrowe see it be not brought

Into the Rochelle to fetch the fumose wine,
Ner into Beytonuse Bay for salt so fine,
What is then Spaine ? What is Flanders also ?
As who sayd, nought, the thrift is agoe.
For the little land of Flanders is
But a staple to other lands ywis :
And all that groweth in Flanders graine and seede
May not a moneth finde hem meate and brede.
What hath then Flanders, bee Flemings lieffe or loth,
But a little Mader and Flemish Cloth :
By Drapering of our wooll in substance
Liven her commons, this is her governance,
Without wich they may not live at ease.
Thus must hem sterve, or with us must have peace.

OF THE COMMODITIES OF PORTUGAL

The Marchandie also of Portugal
By divers lands turne into sale.
Portugalers with us have trouth in hand :
Whose Marchandie commeth much into England.
They ben our friends, with their commodities,
And wee English passen into their countrees.
Her land hath wine, Osey, Ware and Graine,
Figges, Reysins, hony and Cordoweyne :
Dates and Salt, Hides and such Marchandy :
And if they would to Flanders passe by,
They should not bee suffred ones ner twyes,
For supporting of our cruell enemies,
That is to say Flemings with her gyle :
For changeable they are in little while.
Then I conclude by reasons many moe,
If we suffered neither friend nor foe,
What so enemies, and so supporting
Passe for by us in time of werring,
Seth our friends will not ben in cause
Of our hindering, if reson lede this clause :

Then nede from Flanders peace bee to us sought,
And other lands should seeke peace, dout nought :
For Flanders is Staple, as men tell mee,
To all nations of Christianitie.

OF THE COMMODITIES OF THE GENUOYS AND HER GREAT CARACKS

The Genuois comen in sundry wises
Into this land with divers marchandises
I great Caracks, arrayed withouten lacke,
With cloth of gold, silke, and pepper blacke
They brin with them, and of crood great plentee,
Woll Oyle, Woad ashen, by vessel in the see,
Cotton, Rochalum, and good gold of Genne.
And then be charged with wolle againe I wenne,
And wollen cloth of ours of colours all.
And they adventure, as ofte it doth befall,
Into Flanders with such things as they bye,
That is their chiefe staple sekerly :
And if they would be our full enemies,
They should not passe our stremes with merchandise.

THE COMMODITIES AND NICETEES OF THE VENETIANS AND FLORENTINES, WITH THEIR GALLEES

The great Gallees of Venice and Florence
Be well laden with things of complacence,
All spicery and of grossers ware :
With sweete wines all manner of chaffare,
Apes and Japes, and marmusets tayled,
Nifles and trifles that little have avayled :
And things with which they fetely blere our eye :
With things not enduring that we bye.
For much of this chaffare that is wastable
Might be forborne for dere and deceivable.
And that I wene as for infirmaties
In our England are such commodities

Withouten helpe of any other lond
Which by witte and practise both yfound :
That all humors might be voided sure,
Which that we gleder with our English cure :
That we should have no need of Scamonie,
Turbit, enforbe, correct Diagredie,
Rubarbe, Sene, and yet they ben no needefull
But I know things all so speedefull,
That growen here, as those things sayd.
Let of this matter no man be dismayed :
But that a man may voyde infirmatie
Without degrees fet fro beyond the sea.

OF THE COMMODITIES OF BRABANT AND ZEELAND AND HENAULD AND MARCHANDY CARRIED ON LAND TO THE MARTES

Yet marchandy of Brabant and Zeland
The Madre and Woad, that dyers take on hand
To dyen with, Garlike and Onions,
And saltfishe als for husband and commons.
But they of Holland at Caleis byen our felles,
And wolles our, that Englishmen hem selles.
And the chaffare that Englishmen doe byen
In the marts, that noe man may denien,
Is not made in Brabant that countree :
It commeth from out of Henauld, not by see,
But al by land, by carts, and from France,
Bourgoyne, Colein, Cameret in substance.[1]

Such then were the varied cargoes carried by the Hanseatic merchants throughout the years when they were the middlemen in nearly all the business transactions of Northern Europe. The Hansa merchants

[1] *The Principal Voyages of the English Nation*, Hakluyt, Vol. I, p. 181. (Everyman Edition.)

were astute and far-seeing ; their fingers were always on the ever-changing pulse of Europe.

As the taste of the age changed, so the merchandise carried changed too ; when a fresh impulse towards the arts arose, then the great burgher princes of the League turned their thoughts to fine and artistic things.

It is certain that the merchants of these times were one of the main channels through which art, literature and civilization spread over the land. The Hansa never slept ; its wits were constantly at work to sense the new demands and to cater for them ; and a more clever body of traders has never existed.

MONEY-BOX

CHAPTER III

THE DEVELOPMENT OF COINAGE—THE MEDIÆVAL TRADE ROUTES—HANSEATIC SEA LAWS

THE twelfth century saw a very big advance in the condition of trade. Everywhere there was an urge towards development and with it came bettered conditions. For instance, the twelfth century saw the introduction of a credit system which in no small degree did away with the old system of barter, although there was still a large amount of trade on the direct exchange basis—especially when merchants were dealing with the more uncivilized nations.

About this time, too, many countries made an effort to stabilize their coinage ; in those days most of the smaller rulers made a practice of both coining base money and of clipping such coins as came into their hands, and therefore much of the coined money was held in bad repute.

The most trustworthy coinage was that of the Baltic merchants—the Österlings—and that of Lübeck, and merchants began to adopt the habit of demanding payment in these currencies.

One of the oldest systems of European coinage was that of Flanders, whose pound—composed of twenty shillings of twelve groats each—is directly represented in our coinage of to-day.

Payment in bar-silver was occasionally made in the trade of Northern Europe, but barter was more usual with those countries whose civilizations were backward. In various Northern museums may be seen spirals of silver wire which were used as payment during the ninth century, which is known as the " Viking Age "; in some cases these spirals were made of copper thinly coated with silver—so, very early in the history of commerce there was need for acuteness in bargaining. Weights also were often shaved down, and to prevent this they were sometimes made of iron thinly coated with bronze, as by this means any attempt at tampering with them could be easily detected.

It is interesting to note that it was the forbidding of usury by the Church, as founded upon direct Biblical teachings, that thrust the Jews into prominence as the earliest money-lenders, but it was not long before the amazing profits to be gained in this way tempted the Lombards and Italian bankers, and later on the Hanseats, to disregard the religious laws. The most general excuse was that no interest was charged on the loan, but that their profit was demanded as a forfeit for delayed repayment. At the height of its prosperity the Hanseatic League wielded an immense power from its capacity for lending money. As security they frequently took crowns and regalia from the reigning kings who were in need of funds.

Edward III pawned his crown and jewels more than once. There is a record of a commission for receiving the great crown from Conrad Clypping and various other German merchants to whom it was pledged in 1344.[1]

---

[1] Patent Roll 211, membræ 32. Public Record Office.

Another great step on the road to trade facilities was the establishment, in the twelfth century, of a postage system throughout Italy, to be followed, in 1237, by a like system in Germany, thus opening up these countries for the conveyance of letters, bills of sale and merchandise.

Rome, as the headquarters of the Pope, received the enormous taxes levied by the Church ; and, as these dues had always been demanded in coin, money was far more common in the Italian states, and so they were on a far better commercial basis than was the case in the other parts of Europe, where barter and exchange of commodities was still the more usual form of trade.

Thus even in the beginning of the Hansa organization, the Italian cities were in a flourishing condition, and were the rich distributing centres for the Eastern trade.

Venice, in the fourteenth century, the richest town in Europe, possessing a population of almost two hundred thousand, had for hundreds of years been the centre of a valuable salt trade. The widespread demand for this salt led to the founding of a well-organized fleet of boats which, having discharged their cargoes of salt, returned laden with various merchandise. During the Crusades, the Italians had used these ships for conveying men and equipment, and in so doing had amassed very great wealth.

Florence, situated on the main route from Northern Europe to Rome, grew into a renowned banking city ; there lived the Medici family, one of the first and richest families of bankers and money-lenders, a trace of which lingers in this country to this day, for the three

gold balls in the front of our pawnshops are a part of
the arms of the Medici, the first and most flourishing
of pawnbrokers.

Genoa, second only to Venice, specialized in trade
with Tunis, and with the grain-growing lands round
the Black Sea.   Much of its trade was water-carried
round to Marseilles, from whence it was distributed
to the Rhone cities.

But the main stream of goods left Italy through
Venice and was carried over the Brenner, Gothard and
Splügen passes to Innsbruck.   From there there were
two main routes of distribution, the first to Augsburg
(the city made famous by the rich trading house of the
Counts Fugger), Nuremberg, Ulm and Regensburg,
and from thence to the cities of North Germany and the
Baltic ; the second to Basle, and from thence down the
Rhine to Cologne and so to Bruges, which was for many
years the greatest trading centre of Western Europe.

There was a close alliance between Italy and the
South German cities of Augsburg, Nuremberg and
Ulm, and these cities, although they were under the
Hanseatic organization, never entered into such close
relations with it as did the cities of North Germany and
the Baltic.   The Hanseatic Kontor at Venice, the
famous Fondago di Tedeschi, never in any way resem-
bled those of Bergen, Novgorod, Bruges and London.
In fact, the Hanseats in Venice were always under the
strict rule and surveillance of the Italians ; and it is
difficult to understand the attitude of these usually
domineering Hansa merchants towards their Venetian
colleagues.

To turn to the great trade route between the Baltic

and the Black Sea. Early in its history the Hansa established a trading-post at Novgorod, which was situated on the River Volkhov, about two miles below the spot where the river leaves Lake Ilmen; this trading-post, called St. Peter's Court, was one of the most interesting of the Hansa Kontors. Novgorod was the receiving depot for all the Eastern goods that were brought up the Dnieper from the Black Sea, and up the Volga from the Caspian.

From Visby the ships sailed across to the mouth of the Neva, up the river, over Lake Ladoga, up the Volkhov river, across Lake Ilmen, and then up the Lovat river. When this river became unnavigable there was a portage, and this portage was within easy reach of three rivers, the Dnieper, leading down to the Black Sea, and so to the Bosphorus and Constantinople; the Dwina, on the west, running directly into the Baltic; and the Volga on the east leading up into Russia.

These four rivers offered unparalleled water-ways for the spread of trade.

So that there were three great trade routes across Europe:

(1) The route across the Alps, carrying the Italian and Eastern trade to the cities of South Germany, and giving rise to the loose organization of the League in these cities.

(2) The various branch routes from Innsbruck, distributing the goods down the Rhone into France, and down the Rhine into Flanders.

(3) The great trade routes across Russia from the Black Sea to the Baltic.

Across these inland routes passed all the varied merchandise of the times ; either carried, with infinite pain and trouble by boat up the water-ways, with their many arduous land portages, or taken by caravans overland between the various trading-posts. Of course wherever possible water transport was easier, cheaper and safer ; although the land grew considerably more settled as time went on, and the various bodies of merchants made themselves responsible for the upkeep of the roads and the safety of the merchandise carried.

It was no mean undertaking to transport the various classes of trade goods over such vast stretches of country.

As regards the sea transport of merchandise there are existing Hansa records laying down certain laws for the conduct of both the Captains (Patrons) and the merchants' agents (Negociants).

These laws are of interest as giving us an intimate glimpse into the inner working of the League, and it should be noted that they protect not only the merchant but also the sailors. These records of rules were preserved in Lübeck, Stralsund, Wismar and Lüneburg, and also in Hamburg. They are under fifteen heads, and deal with many subjects, including the composition of fleets,[1] the rights of partners, the engagement and discharge of Captains, the engagement and payment of sailors and their liabilities, the preservation

---

[1] The Hansa voyages were almost always undertaken in convoys, there are but few records of a single vessel sailing with a cargo ; the Hansa well understood the mutual protection afforded by the convoy system, both in times of bad weather and in the event of an attack by pirates.

of cargo, shipwreck, attack by pirates (*force majeure*), stranded merchandise, delivery of goods, shipping masters' accounts, behaviour of sailors, and payments extraordinary to sailors.

The following are one or two examples :

THE MARITIME LAWS [1]

" He who intends to go from one port to another should take from the town from which he starts a letter saying where he will go and the nature of his business. When he arrives at his port of discharge he should obtain a letter saying that he has delivered the goods. If he arrive at Bergen or Flanders or England he should then get these letters from the Hanseatic Kontor (received 1369)."

" If a Captain be safe in any port and sees that another Captain cannot, on account of distress, make port, the Captain already in port has the right, if he so think fit, to order his sailors to aid the one in distress to enter harbour. If a sailor shall refuse he is to be deprived of his pay, put ashore, and from thenceforth no other Hansa ship shall hire him."

" If a sailor leave his Captain the latter may, when the man is arrested, if such be his, the Captain's, desire, demand the restitution of all the pay he has received, and also that he do pay for his board. This case to be judged without delay. No Captain to take such a sailor back into his service. (1378.) "

" The Captain who engages sailors for a voyage shall

---

[1] These laws were translated into French by M. Pardessus, who obtained them from Herr M. Lappenberg, the able annotator of Sartorius.

on setting sail pay them one third of the pay agreed upon ; when they arrive at the port of discharge he shall pay them the second third ; on returning to their port of departure he shall pay them the remaining third. If any Captain violate these laws and does not conform to them, he shall pay to his organization a fine of three marks silver."

" If it so happens that several sailors, after receiving their pay, do not come on board at once upon the hour of sailing, and so prevent the hoisting of the sails, or if a sailor deserts (if he be caught) the man shall be liable to the death penalty." [1]

" All Captains who have cargoes of grain must come to an agreement with their sailors and ' bosseman ' [2] to move the cargo as often as it is necessary. If there is any negligence in this respect the Captain to be responsible. Each time of moving the Merchant's Agent to give to the men for each cargo two gros flammans et demi." (Law of 1412, 1417, 1418.)

" In case of ship-wreck the sailors and bossemen must aid the merchant's agent to save the cargo. An equable wage to be given them for so doing. If they should refuse, they shall be charged, judged, and made an example of."

---

[1] Deserters were subjected to various penalties. A law of 1378 merely condemned them to refund their pay and to be expelled from the Hanseatic service ; the above law condemned them to death, but, according to Sartorius, this decision was only arrived at *ad referendum*. Laws of 1418 and 1434 indicate merely imprisonment, and one of 1591 substitutes for " death " " La marque à l'oreille." Authority : Emile Worms.

[2] Bosseman = a low Dutch word signifying pilot, or Contre-maitre. (Author's note.)

" The Towns have decided on the subject of the winter voyages.[1] No merchant of the German League shall set to sea from Martinmas (Nov. 11) to Candlemas (Feb. 2) either to Flanders and the cities there, neither shall he set sail to the West (except for those ships charged with beer, herrings or cod), neither shall any merchant of the League sail East after the prescribed time. If he takes goods from West to East he shall not be allowed to unload or sell them in the towns in the East, and he will have to re-transport them from whence they came. (Decision of 1391 taken *ad referendum*.) "

Beer and herrings might set sail as late as December 6th. In the close time for sailing, small fleets might sail up the rivers for the interior. The penalty for any merchants or Captains disobeying this law was confiscation of the ships and goods. If the Captain or the Merchant's Agent did not belong to a Hansa town, no citizen, or foreigner domiciled in the city (i.e. the port of arrival), might buy his goods or ships on pain of instant confiscation. But if the Captain managed to preserve his fleet no one might demand of him any toll during one year.[2]

In all this widespread trade, and in spite of all the difficulties of transport, the Hansa insisted on goods being of the best quality. All complaints were dealt with at headquarters ; and, if the delinquent were traced, he was very severely dealt with. In fact, after

[1] This also appears in the " Statutes Maritime " of Hamburg in 1276 and in Lübeck in 1299. (Author's note.)
[2] Emile Worms, *Histoire Commerciale de la Ligue Hanséatique*. Paris, 1864.

a series of complaints of bad herrings, packed and transported far inland, the organization elected its own official fish-packers, who were responsible for the size and quality of the fish.

In several instances it is recorded that merchants were heavily fined, and even expelled from the League, for delivering faulty woven goods and furs in bad condition.

On the other hand, the heads of the various Kontors were ordered to exercise every caution in buying goods, especially at such Kontors as St. Peter's Court, Novgorod, where they were trading with barbarians who lacked any idea of trade honour, and were adepts at adulterating their honey, wax and tallow; and in palming off moth-eaten furs on any merchants who knew no better.

Although the Hansa was an extremely astute and clever organization and often sailed very near the wind in matters of diplomacy, all records go to show that they insisted on a high standard in their merchandise, and were not slow to punish any offenders whose sharp practices brought the League into disrepute.

KING COD MASCOT

CHAPTER IV

A LTHOUGH many of the travellers' tales which
achieved such popularity in the thirteenth and
fourteenth centuries have long since been recognized
as a wild mixture of fact and fiction, it would be a great
pity to ignore them ; for, apart from their naïve and
delightful humour, they throw much light on the
various modes of travel, the merchandise carried, and
the trade routes used.

In places, too, they testify to an astonishing amount
of knowledge with which one would scarcely have
credited those early people.

The most popular of these " Travellers' Tales " was
that ascribed to Sire Jehan de Mandeville, who pur-
ported to be an English Knight, born at St. Albans.
It has been proved beyond a doubt that these tales were
not the work of any one man, but were compiled from
various earlier sources, in all probability by a Liégeois,
one Jehan d'Outremeuse. They were first printed
in 1499 by Wynkyn de Worde, and the version I
have used is the excellent edition done from the
Cotton manuscript into modern spelling by A. W.
Pollard.

Setting aside the complicated authorship, the tales
remain—amusing, wonderful in their credulity, and

occasionally striking in their description of the life of the times.

The travels of Sir John Mandeville deal very largely with travel in the East, with the splendours of the Court of the Great Cham and the wonders of the land of Cathay ; with India, the Royal Estate of Prester John and the wild expanse of Tartary.

To Mandeville's tales may be added the journals of Friar Oderic and Friar William de Rubruquis, who travelled in the years 1246 and 1253 respectively and who provided the mythical Mandeville with a great part of his information.

The first part of the following extracts I have selected for their interest and the light they throw on mediæval trade and travelling ; and the second part for their amusing admixture of fact and fiction.

" In that land [1] ne in many other beyond that, no man may see the Star Transmontane, that is clept the Star of the Sea, that is unmoveable and that is toward the north, that we celp the Lode-star. But men see another star, the contrary to him, that is towards the South, that is clept Antartic. And right as the ship-men take their advice here and govern them by the Lode-star, right so do ship-men beyond those parts by the Star of the South, the which star appeareth not to us. And this star that is towards the North, that we clepe the Lode-star, ne appeareth not to them. For which cause men may well perceive, that the land and the sea be of round shape and form ; for the part of the firmament sheweth in one country that sheweth not in an other country. And men may well prove by experience and subtle compass-ment of wit, that if a man found passages by ships

[1] Sumatra. (Author's note.)

that would go to search the world, men might go by ship all about the world and above and beneath.

" The which thing I prove thus, after that I have seen. For I have been towards the parts of Brabant and beholden the Astrolabe [1] that the star that is clept the Transmontane is fifty-three degrees high; and more further in Almayne and Bohemia it hath fifty-eight degrees ; and more further towards the parts Septentrional it is sixty-two degrees of height and certain minutes ; for I myself have measured it with the Astrolabe. Now shall ye know, that against the Transmontane is the tother star that is clept Antartic, as I have said before. And those two stars ne move never, and by them turneth all the firmament right as doth a wheel that turneth by his axle-tree. So that those stars bear the firmament in two equal parts, so that it hath as much above as it hath beneath. After this, I have gone towards the parts meridional, that is, towards the South, and I have found that in Lybia men see first the Star Antartic. And so far I have gone more further in those countries, that I have found that star more high ; so that towards the high Lybia it is eighteen degrees of height and certain minutes (of the which sixty minutes makes a degree)." [2]

The following passage points to a direct trade route from the East up the Volga to Novgorod, and the Baltic ; or across the short portage to the Don, and down the Don to the Black Sea :

" The region lying beyond Tanais [3] is a very goodly country, having store of rivers and woods towards

[1] An instrument for taking astronomical observations. (Author's note.)

[2] *Travels of Sir John Mandeville*, edited by A. W. Pollard, pp. 120, 121.

[3] Don. (Author's note.)

the North part thereof. There be mighty huge woods
which two sorts of people do inhabit. One of them is
called Moxel,[1] being mere pagans and without law.
They had neither towns nor cities but only cottages
in the woods. . . . They have abundance of hogs,
and great store of honey and wax, and divers sorts
of rich and costly skins, and plenty of falcons. Next
unto them are other people called Merclas, which the
Latins call Merdui, and they are Saracens. Beyond
them is the river Etilia or Volga, which is the mightiest
river that I ever saw. And it issueth from the North
part of Bulgaria the greater, and so trending along
Southward, disimboqueth into a certain lake [2] containing in circuit the space of four months' travel,
whereof I will speak hereafter. The two aforesaid
rivers, namely Tanais and Etilia otherwise called
Volga, towards the northern regions through which
we travelled, are not distant asunder above ten days
journey, but southward they are divided a great space
one from another. For Tanais descendeth into the
Sea of Pontus [3] Etilia maketh the aforesaid sea or
lake, with the help of many rivers which fall thereinto
out of Persia." [4]

" Then put they us to our choice, whether we
would have carts and oxen, or pack horses to transport our carriages. And the merchants of Constantinople advised me not to take carts of the citizens
of Soldaia but to buy covered carts of mine own (such
as the Russians carry their skins in) and to put all our
carriages, which I would daily take out, into them ;
because if I should use horses, I must be constrained

[1] Wild tribes living beyond the Don. (Author's note.)
[2] The Caspian Sea. (Author's note.)
[3] The Black Sea. (Author's note.)
[4] *Travels of Sir John Mandeville*, edited by A. W. Pollard, pp.
292, 293.

at every bait to take down my carriages, and to lift
them up again onto sundry horses' backs ; and besides, that I should ride a more gentle pace, by the
oxen drawing the carts. Wherefore contenting myself with their evil counsel, I was travelling unto
Sartach two months which I could have done in one,
if I had gone by horse. I brought with me from
Constantinople, (being by the merchants advised so
to do) pleasant fruits, muscadel wine and delicate
biscuit bread to present unto the Governours of
Soldaia, to the end I might obtain free passage ;
because they look favourably upon no man which
cometh with an empty hand. All of which things I
bestowed in one of my carts (not finding the Governours of the City at home) for they told me, if I could
carry them to Sartach that they would be most acceptable unto him. We took our journey therefore about
the Kalends of June with four covered carts of our
own, and with two other which we borrowed of them,
wherein we carried our bedding to rest upon in the
night, and they allowed us five horse to ride upon,
for there were just five persons in our company ;
namely I myself and mine associate, Friar Bartholomew
of Cremona, and Goset, the bearer of these presents,
the man of God Turgemannus, and Nicolas, my
servant, whom I bought at Constantinople with some
of the alms bestowed upon me. Moreover they
allowed us two men, which drove our carts and gave
attendance unto our oxen and horses. There be high
promontories on the sea shore from Kersova unto
the mouth of the Tanais. Also there are forty castles
between Kersova and Soldaia, every one of which
almost have their proper language, amongst whom
there were many Goths who spake the Dutch tongue
. . . towards the borders of the said province there
be many great lakes ; upon the banks whereof are
salt pits or fountains, the waters of which so soon as

it entereth into the lake become a hard salt like unto ice, and out of those salt pits Baatu and Sartach have great revenues. For they repair thither out of all Russia for salt and for each cart-load they give two webs of cotton amounting to the value of half a yperpera." [1]

From the above passage it is clear that the German merchants had penetrated as far as the regions round the mouth of the Don as early as 1257, when Friar William de Rubruquis was travelling on behalf of King Louis IX. And it is also interesting to see that the Church had no objection to its priors spending the alms they begged in the purchase of slaves in the markets of Constantinople.

" This emperor [2] may dispend as much as he will without estimation ; for he not dispendeth ne maketh no money but of leather imprinted or of paper. And of that money is some of greater price and some of less price, after the diversity of his statutes. And when that money hath run so long that it begineth to waste then men bear it to the emperor's treasury and then they take new money for the old. And that money goeth throughout all the country and throughout all his provinces, for there and beyond them they make no money neither of gold nor of silver and therefore he may dispend enough and outrageously." [3]

The following extracts are more amusing than convincing ; but they are striking, as they proclaim the

[1] *Travels of Sir John Mandeville*, edited by A. W. Pollard, pp. 264, 265.

[2] The Cham of Cathay. (Author's note.)

[3] *Travels of Sir John Mandeville*, edited by A. W. Pollard, p. 156.

vividness of the travellers' interest and quest for knowledge, together with their evident credulity :

" Between the city of Arkez and the city of Raphnae [1]
there is a river that is called Sabatory ; for on the
Saturday it runs fast and all the week else it stands
still and runs not, or else but fairly.

" Also in Cairo . . . there is a common house
in that city all full of small furnaces, and thither
bring the women of the town their eyren (eggs) of
hens, of geese and of ducks for to be put into those
furnaces.   And they that keep that house cover them
with heat of horse dung without hen, goose or duck
or any other fowl.   And at the end of three weeks
or of a month they come again and take their chickens
and nourish them and bring them forth that all the
country is full of them.   And so men do there both
summer and winter."

" And in that country [2] be white hens without
feathers but they bear white wool as sheep do here." [3]

" Towards the East part of Prester John's land is
an isle good and great, than men clepe Taprobane.
. . .   In this isle be great hills of gold that pismires
(ants) keep full diligently.   And they fine the pured
gold and cast away the unpured gold.   And these
pismires be great as hounds, so that no man dare
come to those hills for the pismires would assail them
and devour them anon.   So that no man may get of
that gold, but by great sleight, and therefore when it
is great heat the pismires rest them in the earth from
prime of the day until noon.   And then the folk of
the country take camels, dromedaries and horses and

---

[1] In Palestine.   (Author's note.)

[2] Canton.   (Author's note.)

[3] *Travels of Sir John Mandeville*, edited by A. W. Pollard, pp.
33, 83 and 136.

other beasts, and go thither, and charge them in all haste that they may ; and after that they flee away in all haste that the beasts may go, or the pismires come out of the earth. And in other times, when it is not so hot and the pismires ne rest them not in the earth, then they get gold by this subtlety. They take mares that had young colts or foals and lay upon the mares void vessels made therefor, they be all open above and hanging low to the earth. And then they send forth those mares for to pasture among those hills and withhold the colts from them at home. And when the pismires see those vessels they leap in anon ; and they have this kind that they let nothing be empty among them, but anon they fill it, be it what manner of thing that it be ; so they fill those vessels with gold. And when that the folk suppose that these vessels be full they put forth anon the young foals, and make them neigh after their dams. And then anon the mares return towards their foals with their charges of gold. And then men discharge them, and get gold enough by this subtlety. For the pismires will suffer beasts to go an pasture among them but no man in no wise." [1]

" And there groweth a manner of fruit as though it were gourds. And when they be ripe, men cut them a-two, and men find within a little beast, in flesh, in bone, and in blood, as though it were a little lamb without wool, and men eat both the fruit and the beast. And that is a great marvel. That fruit I have eaten, although it were wonderful but that I know well that God is marvelous in his works. And, natheles, I told them of as great a marvel to them, that is among us, and that was of the Bernakes. For I told them that in our country were trees that bear fruit that become birds flying, and those that fell in

[1] *Travels of Sir John Mandeville*, edited by A. W. Pollard, p. 198.

the water live, and they that fall upon earth die anon and they be right good to man's meat." [1]

It is interesting to compare the same tale in the German of Friar Odoric; he ends up with:

" even as I myself have heard reported, that there stands certain trees upon the shore of the Irish Sea, bearing fruit like unto a gourd, which at a certain time of the year do fall into the water, and become birds called Bernacles, and this is most true."

" And by all Inde be a great plenty of cockodrills, that is a maner of long serpent, . . . and in the night they dwell on the water and in the day upon the land in rocks and in caves. And they eat no meat in all the winter, but they lie as in a dream, as do the serpents. These serpents slay men, and they eat them weeping; and when they eat they move the over-jaw and not the nether-jaw, and they have no tongue. . . . There also be many beasts that be clept orafles, [2] in Arabia they be clept gerfaunts, that is a beast, pomely or spotted, that is but little more high than is a steed, but he hath the neck a twenty cubits long; his croop and his tail is as of an hart, and he may look over a great high house. And there be also in that country many camles; and is a little beast as a goat, that is wild, and he liveth by the air and eat nought nay drinketh nought at no time. And he changeth his colour oftentime, for men see him often sithes, now in one colour, now in another colour; and he may change him into all manner colours that him list, save only into red and white. . . . And there be also urchins as great as wild swine here; we clep them Porcz de Spine. And there be lions all white, great and mighty. And there also be other beasts as

[1] *Travels of Sir John Mandeville*, edited by A.W. Pollard, p. 174.
[2] Giraffes. (Author's note.)

great and more greater than is a destrier, and men clepe them Loerancs ; and some men clepe them odenthos ; And they have a black head and three long horns trenchant, in the front, sharp as a sword, and the body is slender ; and he is a full felonious beast and he chaseth and slayeth the elephant. . . . And there be also mice as great as hounds, and yellow mice as great as ravons. And there be geese, all red, three sithes more great than ours here. And they have the head, the neck and the breast all black." [1]

" In one of these isles be folk of great stature, as giants. And they be hideous for to look upon. And they have but one eye, and that is in the middle of the front. And they eat nothing but raw flesh and raw fish. And in another isle towards the South dwell folk of foul stature and of cursed kind that have no heads. And their eyen be in their shoulders. . . . And in another isle be folk of foul fashon and shape that have the lip above the mouth so great, that when they sleep in the sun they cover all the face with that lip. . . . And in another isle be folk that go upon their hands and their feet as beasts. And they be all skinned and feathered, and they will leap as lightly into trees, and from tree to tree, as it were squirrels or apes." [2]

I will conclude my chapter of Travellers' Tales with a short extract from the Journal of Johannes de Plano Carpini, who was sent on a mission into Tartary with other Minorite Friars, in 1246, by Pope Innocent IV.

This short passage testifies at least to the accuracy of the Friar's observation :

[1] *Travels of Sir John Mandeville*, edited by A. W. Pollard, pp. 190, 191.
[2] Ibid., pp. 133 and 134.

" The Mongals or Tartars in outward shape, are unlike to all other people. For they are broader between the eyes, and the balls of their cheeks, than men of other nations be. They have flat and small noses, little eyes, and eyelids standing straight upright, they are shaven upon the crown, like priests. They wear their hair somewhat longer about their ears than upon their foreheads ; but behind they let it grow long like women's hair, whereof they braid two locks, binding each of them behind either ear. They have short feet also. The garments as well of the men, as of their women, are all of one fashion. They use neither cloaks, hats nor capes. But they wear jackets framed after a strange manner, of buckram, scarlet, or baldikins. Their Shoubes or gowns are hairy on the outside, and open behind, with tails hanging down to their hams. They use not to wash their garments, neither will in any wise suffer them to be washed especially in the time of thunder. Their habitations be round and cunningly made with wickers and staves in manner of a tent. But in the midst of the tops thereof, they have a window open to convey the light in and the smoke out, for their fire is always in the midst. Their walls be covered with felt. Their doors are made of felt also. Some of these tabernacles may quickly be taken asunder, and set together again, and are carried upon beasts backs. Other some cannot be taken asunder, but are stowed upon carts, and whithersoever they go, be it either to war or to any other place, they transport their tabernacles with them. They are very rich in cattle, as in camels, oxen, sheep and goats. And I think they have more horses and mares than all the world besides. But they have no kine nor other beasts. Their Emperors, their Dukes and other of their nobles do abound with silk, gold, silver and precious stones. Their victuals are all things that may be eaten ; for we saw some of them eat lice. They drink milk in great quantity, but especially mare's milk if they have it. They seeth mill also in water, making it so thin that they may drink thereof. Everyone of them drinks off a cupfull or two in the morning, and sometime they eat nought else all the day long. But in the evening each man hath a little flesh given him to eat, and they drink the broth thereof. Howbeit in summertime, when they have mare's milk enough, they seldom eat flesh, unless perhaps it be given them, or they take some bird or beast in hunting." [1]

[1] *Travels of Sir John Mandeville*, edited by A. W. Pollard, pp. 215, 216.

SEAL OF NOVGOROD

CHAPTER V

NEAR the present-day fishing port of Wollin, on
the island of Wollin, the most easterly of the
islands in the mouth of the Oder, stood the ancient
City of Wollin, the great trading city of the Wends.
In the Norse sagas it is spoken of as Jom, and we are
told that the harbour of Jom could shelter three
hundred ships. The Germans called the city Vineta
—the city of the Wends.

The time of its greatest prosperity was in the tenth
and eleventh centuries, when it was the centre of a vast
and prosperous trade. In 970, the Norsemen settled
on the island and built a great fort which they called
Jomsborg. In 1076 Adam of Bremen, in whose writings fact and fiction take almost equal place, calls it
" the greatest and most glorious city of Europe." He
tells how its streets resounded to the tread of all manner
of people, among them Greeks (by which he means
Russians, so called from their adherence to the Greek
Orthodox Church).

In 1184 Vineta was sacked by the Danes, which
probably gave rise to the legend of the loss of the City,
to be found in all Scandinavian, German and Baltic
literature.

The following is the Legend, which I have translated from the Swedish of Valborg Olander, adjunkt of the Seminary at Falun.

LEGEND OF THE LOST VINETA

Off the north-east coast of the island of Usedom, one can see, if the weather be fine and the sea calm, the ruins of a vast old city. It was once the famous city of Vineta, which more than a thousand years ago suffered such grievous punishment for its sins. Vineta was greater than any other city in Europe, even greater than the mighty and magnificent city of Constantinople; in it dwelt all manner of folk—Greeks, Slavs, Wends, Saxons and many others. Each kept his own religion, but the Saxons, who were Christians, dared not openly declare their faith, for the heathen gods were publicly worshipped.

But despite their heathen worship, the dwellers in Vineta were honourable and clean living, and in hospitality and friendliness towards strangers they were unequalled.

They carried on a vast trade, their storehouses were filled with the most wonderful and precious objects, and each year there came ships full of merchants from every country, yes—even from the farthest corners of the earth.

Therefore the most amazing riches poured into the town, till the folk knew not what to do with them. The city gates were of bronze and copper, and the bells were of silver, and that metal was so common that the people used it even for their everyday household utensils ; while the children in the streets played with shining plates of the precious metal.

But, through its riches, the dwellers in Vineta fell into woeful and sinful pride. Therefore they were smitten by God's just wrath. The mighty town fell a prey to the rushing and hungry waters. Then came the Swedes from Gotland with many ships, and took back with them all that they could fish up from the sea of the town's great riches. Much gold and silver, copper and pewter, and the loveliest of marble did they take away ; also the great copper gates they carried back to Visby, to which town all the trade of Vineta now passed.

The spot where Vineta stood is visible even to this day. If one travels from Wolgast over Peene to the island of Usedom, so opposite Dammerow-Kozeroff plain, twelve miles from Wolgast, if the sea is calm— deep, deep down in the water one can see marble pillars and stone foundations. It is the ruins of Vineta, stretching from east to west. The streets are marked by cobble-stones, large stones show the remains of the houses, some reach yards up into the water—there stood the churches and law-courts ; others lie in perfect order, just like well-laid foundations, so it is easy to see where new houses would have stood, if the waves had not swallowed up the city.

In the sunken town there are still signs of life. When the water is calm one can see strange things. Tall, lonely figures, in long pleated gowns, wander up and down the streets ; often they sit in carriages of gold or astride fine black horses ; sometimes they are glad and merry ; sometimes they walk in long sad processions, and one sees that they bear a coffin to burial. On still, calm evenings one can hear the silver bells of

the city ringing for vespers ; and, on Easter night—
for the ruin of Vineta was accomplished between Good
Friday and Easter—one can see the whole city as it was
in its prime. As a punishment for its pride and
wickedness it rises up like a warning spectre with all
its houses and churches, its gates and bridges and
towers, plain to be seen.

But at night or in stormy weather, no ship dare
venture near the ruins lest it be cast against the cliffs
and shattered to splinters, and all on board lose their
lives.

From the adjacent village of Loddin an old road still
runs towards the ruins—and the folk have called that
road, from time immemorial, the road to Vineta !

Some versions of the legend add that, if anyone who
beholds the lost city on the night of its appearance
can pay for any article, offered so eagerly by the merchants, in money—let it be even the smallest coin—
then the proud Vineta might stay up above the waves,
and take once more its proper place among the
great trading cities of the world.

Like the sunk Atlantis, legend and story have surrounded the lost Vineta, but the fate of Wollin was far
more prosaic than legend would have us believe.

After its sack by the Danes, it was burnt by
Canute VI in 1183, and we hear of it again as being
attacked by the Swedes in 1630, and again by the
Brandenburghers in 1659 ; so Wollin existed, and
had a certain amount of history up to quite a late
date.

That is the legend of Vineta, but there was another

town not so far away, that had an equally romantic and
stirring history, and it was real and not legendary.

The first great Hanseatic city was to rise to fame
outside the country of the League's inception. That
was the city of Visby, on the island of Gotland.

The geographical position of the island made it an
extremely suitable spot for the founding of a trading
centre for ships creeping round the Baltic coasts.
Starting from Lübeck they could follow the coast-line
to the island of Rügen, then cross to Bornholm, from
thence to Öland and on to Gotland—and from there
cross to the Gulfs of Riga or Finland, without ever
having to face the dangers of being out of sight of land
for very long. The position of Visby on Gotland
points to its having been established as a half-way
house for traders passing by sea between Russia and
Scandinavia and Western Europe.

It was this excellent sea route, and the presence of
the big water-ways—the Neva opening into the Gulf
of Finland ; the Dwina opening into the Gulf of Riga ;
the Vistula opening into the Gulf of Danzig ; together
with the Oder and the Elbe—which led to the foundation of so many League cities in that part of the country.
The most important of these were Danzig, Stralsund,
Rostock, Wismar, Trävemunde and Lübeck—the latter
was to rise to the position of head of the Hanseatic
League after the fall of Visby.

The island of Gotland always maintained a position
of great independence. It possessed its own Gotland
Law, which it administered itself, and it paid only a
voluntary tribute of sixty marks silver to its Swedish
suzerains. There is evidence that this Gotland Law

was extended by privilege to the many foreign merchants living in the city.

Some authorities, among them Professor Björkander, endeavour to prove that Visby had little or no history before the time of the Lübeck merchants in the middle of the twelfth century, and that, in fact, it was a city founded entirely by German merchants ; but this theory does not bear close examination. Of late years much historical and archæological research has been done in and around Visby, and enough material has been discovered to prove, beyond doubt, that Visby had a flourishing trade as far back as the Viking Age, long before the Lübeck merchants, tempted by the riches of the city, and the paying fish trade in the Baltic, turned envious eyes towards Gotland, and, by using their famous diplomacy, obtained for themselves privileges which put them on a sufficiently firm footing to enable them gradually to make themselves masters of the city.

We have no evidence that the people of Visby ever looked askance at the Hanseatic merchants, on the contrary they probably welcomed them for their un-doubted skill in all matters of commerce. A long history of trade had brought Visby into contact with many foreigners and the prominent burghers knew full well the prosperity that came in the wake of foreign trade.

It was from the eleventh to the fourteenth centuries that Visby was at the height of its prosperity.

An amazing number of coins have been dug up in and around the city, and these alone are evidence of its commercial importance. The coins found are of all nationalities : Arabic and Byzantine (a proof of trade carried on with the East via Novgorod, the Russian and German water-ways and Italy), Roman, Danish, Swedish, Russian, German, Irish and Anglo-Saxon—the latter minted in Exeter, Lincoln, Hereford and York prior to the Norman Conquest.

The Hanseatic Kontors established in those cities where the League had its headquarters differed very greatly in character, but everywhere they were ruled by the same strict and binding laws. The Kontor at Visby was centred round the magnificent church of Maria Teutonicorum, and, as was the custom in those times, the church was used for various secular purposes. There, the heads of the League—burgher representatives from Visby, Lübeck, Soest and Dortmund—kept their money, papers and records, and the seals that were used in all transactions of the League. They were the acting administrators for the great organization, and their word was law, and their power supreme. There were two seals used at Visby, one for the resident German merchants, whose inscription ran—" Sigillum Theutonicorum in Gotlandia manentium " ; and one for the travelling merchants—" Sigillum Theutonicorum Gotlandia freqentanicum."

In no other town which has survived in some part from those old Hanseatic days can one see such perfect examples of Hanseatic burgher architecture. Not that there are remains of wonderful civic buildings in Visby, as there are in Lübeck or Danzig ; but there are standing, to this day, many of the old crow-stepped houses, almost as they were in the time of the city's pride and glory.

The best example is the old Hanseatic house in Strandgatan, called the Gamla Apotek ; it is a perfect specimen, with its crow-stepped gables, the peculiar false front to the upper story, and its massive cellars, where many a fine vintage has been stored ! The most striking merchant feature is the row of " hoist-doors," one above the other in the centre, through which the merchandise was hauled up to the different stories.

Another interesting proof of the important part played in the city by the German merchants survived in the name given to a small market in the town. It was called the " Roland market," doubtless from the fact that a statue of Roland stood there. These statues of Roland prove the popularity of the Legend of Roland and the Twelve Paladins of Charlemagne current throughout Germany, and, in the Danish version of the Karla Magnus Saga, throughout Scandinavia. In a privilege granted to Bremen in IIII mention is made of a " Statua Rolandi " which was probably erected as a symbol of the city's judicial rights.

In the time of its greatness Visby was certainly a magnificent city. The houses were richly and beautifully decorated, the overhanging gables carved and painted, and inlaid with marble. Inside the houses there was still more evidence of the riches of the Visby merchants. There is mention of copper doors, copper and silver window-frames, richly stamped leather wall-hangings and upholstery, and table services of gold and silver ; while so great was the pomp and extravagance of the merchant classes that the Hanseatic League was obliged to draw up sumptuary laws forbidding the

wearing of certain stuffs, and, and this clause is not the
least amusing, limiting the number of dishes served at
a burgher wedding to eighty ! Surely this would be
considered a generous number even for our day, which
we are so prone to label as extravagant !

After the absorption of Visby by the Hanseatic
League it had a very close association with London.
The Steelyard in Thames Street, close to Blackfriars,
the English Kontor of the Hanseatic League, was the
storehouse of the Visby merchants, and was known in
its earliest days as the Hall of the Easterlings—i.e.
Österlings—another name for Gotlanders, signifying
the dwellers by the Östsjö or Baltic.

But the associations with England did not stop short
at the Steelyard ; in two other things we had, and still
have, a close connection with this past city of the
Baltic. One was our coinage and the other our Sea
Laws.

To this day our coinage is reminiscent of the island
of Gotland, for our shilling is but the " skilling " of
the Visby merchants, and our word sterling is
nothing more or less than a corruption of the word
" Österling."

The place taken by Visby in sea law is extremely
interesting, and proves, as nothing else could, the
enormous power and influence wielded by the
Hanseatic merchants of that city.

The Visby Sea Law was derived from the Sea Law
of Oleron, and was probably first drawn up from three
codes, those of Oleron, Lübeck and Amsterdam. The
first known text is preserved in the Lübeck archives,
written in Old Saxon about 1240 ; its title is " Water-

recht dat de Kooplüds en de Schiffers gemakt hetten to Visby "—the Sea Laws drawn up by the Merchants and Seamen of Visby.

The first printed copy was made by Godfrey de Gemen in Copenhagen in 1505.

The Sea Laws of Oleron, from which the Visby Law was mainly taken, are of considerable antiquity, but the exact manner in which they came to be assembled is not very clear.

One Cleirac, a member of the Bordeaux government, in his book, *Les Us et Coustumes de la Mer* (1647), states that Eleanor of Aquitaine, wife of the English King Henry II, ordered the judgments of the big maritime court of the Island of Oleron, off Rochelle, to be collected and arranged, after her journey to the Holy Land, when she accompanied her husband on the Second Crusade, where she had seen how much venerated was the Book of the Consulate of the Sea, then in use in the Levantine Ports.

There is an account of Le Laye Oleroun coming to England in *De Superioritate Maris Angliæ*, which may be consulted in the Public Record Office ; and an early copy in early fourteenth-century text is preserved under the title *La Charte D'Oleroun des Juggements de la Mier*, in the Liber Memorandorum and the Liber Horn, in the archives of the Guildhall, London.

The first translation into English would seem to have been made by Thomas Petyte in 1536, in *Rutter of the Sea* ; but prior to that there had been a Flemish version made in the latter part of the fourteenth century, and preserved in The Purple Book of Bruges, in the archives of that city ; the title is *Dit es en Coppie van den Rollen*

van Oleron van den Vonesse van der Zee, and the names
in the old usages are changed to the names of Flemish
ports.

In the maritime port of Danzig there is a fifteenth-
century copy, in Flemish, entitled *Dit is Twater Recht
in Vlaenderen.*

And so the laws passed round the Baltic in the
recognized trade routes ; but how they came by their
name of Visby Sea Laws, and how they came to be
recognized as such, as far away from the Baltic as
England and Scotland, is a thing that still puzzles the
most recognized authorities.

The Laws and Customs of the Sea cover a very wide
field and contain judgments in cases of Shipwreck,
Jettison of Cargo, Responsibilities of Masters, Damage
to Ships, Disputes with Sailors, Cases of Illness, Feed-
ing of Crews, etc.—in fact, they deal with almost every
emergency that could arise at sea.

The following is an Index of the twenty-four Laws,
and from it one can see with what care and judgment
they were drawn up. I am afraid that space forbids
me to do more than quote one or two of the shorter,
and more original ones.

The text used is the Liber Horn, which is preserved
in the Guildhall, London ; and the Old French text,
together with an English translation, may be consulted
in The Black Book of the Admiralty.

As a matter of interest I give the first Law in the Old
French :

" Ceo est la copie de la chartre Doleroun des juge-
mentz de la meer. Premierement lem fet un homme
mestre dune nef. La nef est a deus hommes ou a

trois. La nef sen part du pays dount ele est et vient a Burdeux ou a la Rochelle ou aillours et se treite a aler en pais estraunge a Le Mestre ne poet pas vendre la nef sill nad comaundment ou procuracion des seigneurs mes si il ad mestier de depenses il pout ben mettre ascunes des apparailes en gage par coumseil des compaignouns de la nef, et ceo est le jugement en ceo cas."

(1) The Master shall not sell the ship, but may pledge the ship's apparel to buy necessaries.

(2) The Master is bound to take counsel with the ship's company as to whether he shall set sail or not.

(3) The duties of the Master and Mariners in a case of shipwreck.

(4) In case of shipwreck the Master may carry forward the goods in another ship.

(5) The Mariners may not go ashore whilst in Harbour without the permission of the Master.

(6) Mariners who go ashore unless in the service of the ship and are hurt, must be cured at their own expense.

(7) A sick Mariner must be placed ashore in charge of a nurse, and if he dies, his wages must be paid to his widow or relatives.

(8) The Master in case of danger may make jettison, how the latter is to be shared between the ship and the cargo.

(9) If the Master has to cut away his mast he is to be compensated in case of jettison.

(10) The quality of the ropes to be used in handling the cargo should be approved by the merchants.

(11) To what extent the Master is liable to make compensation for damage to the cargo through careless stowing.

(12) Penalty for abusive language and for blows on board ship.

(13) Harbour pilotage to be payable by the owners of the cargo.

(14) Disputes on board ship between the Master and Mariners.

(15) Damage done to a ship at her moorings by another ship entering port.

(16) A ship should not anchor too near to another ship lying in a shallow harbour. All anchors to be buoyed.

(17) What diet the Mariners of Brittany and Normandy should be given.

(18) What freight should be allotted to the Mariners.

(19) The Mariners are bound to bring the ship back to port.

(20) Distinction between Mariners hired for freight and those hired for wages.

(21) Mariners may take meat ashore but not drink.

(22) Demurrage payable by Merchants, how divisible between the Master and the Mariners.

(23) The Master may sell part of the cargo to buy necessaries.

(24) The duty of the Pilot to bring the ship safe to her berth.

From the above I have selected the following five laws as being of particular general interest:

(2) The Master must take the advice of the majority of the ship's company with regard to setting sail; if he does not he is responsible for any loss and must make it good.

(5) A ship departing from port laden, or empty, and arriving at another port, the mariners shall not go ashore without the permission of the Master. For if by any accident the ship should be lost then they would be compelled to make compensation, if they have the wherewithal. But if the ship be in place where she has been moored with four hausers (de

quatre amarees) they may go ashore and return in time for their ship. And this is the judgment in this case.

(6) Mariners hire themselves out to their master and some of them go ashore without leave and get drunk and make a disturbance (fount contekes) and some be hurt. The Master is not under obligation to have them healed . . . he may put them ashore and hire others in their place.

(7) If Mariners be sick (or hurt in the business of the Master) he shall send him ashore, give him a candle and a ship's boy to tend him, or engage a nurse (louer une femme qe prenge garde a li).

(17) The Mariners of the coast of Brittany shall have but one cooked meal a day (qe une quisine le jour) for that they have wine both going and coming. Those of Normandy shall have two for that their Master gives them but water in going. But when the ship reaches the land where the wine grows,[1] the Mariners shall have to drink, and the Master shall provide it.

The following are three short extracts from the *Customs of the Sea*, the text used being a translation from the Old Spanish in The Black Book of the Admiralty, III, 55. These Customs of the Sea are long and detailed and deal with every conceivable subject from " Goods damaged by rats, having no cat on board " to " Fear on the part of the Merchant ; The Mariner who throws away his food designedly ; and the Mariner who strips himself."

CXXV. " A Mariner ought not to undress himself if he is not in a port of wintering. And if he does so, for each time, he ought to be plunged into the sea with a rope from the Yard-arm, three times ; and after three times offending he ought to lose his salary and the goods that he has in the ship."

---

[1] Bruges MS., " de wyn groeyt."

CXXXI. " Further, a Mariner is bound, if he is in charge of the boat, to put persons on shore, and to take off his breeches for that purpose. And if he does not do so, or is not willing to do so, he ought to pay all expenses which any person incurs.

CXXXIII. " Further, the Mariner is bound to take on board the arms which he has agreed upon with the Master of the ship, and if he does not take them on board, the managing owner may purchase them on account of his wages without the consent of the Mariner and the ship's clerk ought to be present." [1]

---

[1] *The Black Book of the Admiralty*, III, 55. Edited by Sir Travers Twist.

ROSTOCK CITY SEAL

CHAPTER VI

AFTER the christianizing of the Danes in the tenth
and eleventh centuries by the German Knights,
the ruling powers in Germany had exercised a certain
amount of authority over the Danish King, so it had
been easy for the German merchants to obtain special
privileges in the trading-posts and towns round the
Baltic, and among the flourishing fishing centres on
the peninsula of Scånia, which was then under Danish
suzerainty.

The middle of the twelfth century saw the Hansa
fairly established in the Baltic cities and participating
to the full in the herring fishing industry and in the
" carrying trade " ; but, as the power of Germany
declined, its hold over Denmark grew tenuous, and it
only required a strong and forceful King in the person
of the Great Valdemar (1157–1182) to stir the Danish
people into revolt against these German merchants,
whose one desire was to obtain and preserve a monopoly
wherever they traded, and who offered no reciprocal
privileges. Trading, as the League did, round and
across the Baltic, the Danes had every opportunity for
harrying the merchant ships, and so great was their
daring and audacity that, after suffering many insults,

the League found itself faced with the necessity of making war.

It was the flourishing trade between Lübeck and Scånia that provoked attack by Valdemar the Great, who, after seizing many of the German trading ships, invaded Holstein and captured Hamburg, after which he turned his attention to Lübeck. With the rise of Denmark, Lübeck entered into a period of great unrest. Attracted by its ever-increasing trade and riches, the neighbouring provinces of Schleswig-Holstein, Mecklenburg and Ratzenberg made constant efforts to seize the city; but its worst enemy was Valdemar, and in 1203 Lübeck fell into the hands of Denmark, to whom she belonged for twelve years and from whom she was only delivered by a clever strategy.

Once rid of the Danes the League Cities banded themselves together and attacked the Danish forces, winning their first victory at the battle of Bornhöved, in 1227. This battle was an important event in the history of Lübeck, for, after their success, the city sent an embassy to the Emperor Frederick II, asking for a confirmation of the privileges given them by Frederick Barbarossa.

He not only consented to do this, but he sent them two charters, one confirming their ancient privileges and the other declaring them a " Free City " for ever, owing allegiance to none but the Emperor. Thus Lübeck became the first free city in the country, and this was of inestimable value to the Hanseatic League, when, after the fall of Visby, its headquarters were removed to the lovely city on the Träve.

But the Danes still continued to harry the Lübeck

merchants, and again in 1249 they were drawn into another fight, and this time it was Lübeck who, almost by its own unaided efforts, won a naval victory over the forces of Eric II, whose ships had been constantly interfering with their carrying trade.

By this time the Baltic carrying trade almost rivalled the fishing industry as a source of riches. There was a constant interchange of merchandise between Visby and Novgorod, where all the traders of the East gathered at the great fairs, to barter their Oriental goods for the rich furs of Russia and the manufactured goods imported by the Hansa.

The Hansa did their utmost to exclude all foreigners —Flemish, Dutch, English and Scandinavians—from participating in this trade, just as they tried, and succeeded, in obtaining for themselves a monopoly in the herring trade ; so the interference of the Danes seriously damaged their trade.

One must always remember that the power of the Scandinavian countries was much weakened by the fact that they were not united—on the contrary they were constantly at war one with the other—and this state of affairs was very favourable to the policy of the League, for it is safe to say that a United Scandinavia would have driven the Hanseatic League out of the Baltic cities and have deprived them of the flourishing fish monopoly and the extensive carrying trade, without which they would probably never have attained to any greatness.

In this first crisis the famous Hansa diplomacy was of very little use to the League, for the Danes had not the slightest respect for treaty rights or privilege charters, and, the moment it was to their interest to throw them over, away they went as if they had never existed.

It was with great reluctance that the Hansa turned to war—they were essentially a peace-loving organization : that policy was far better for trade—but, in the event of war being the only solution of their difficulties, they did not scruple to call upon their large reserves of men and money.

With the accession to the Danish throne, in 1326, of Valdemar III, then a boy of twelve, afterwards called Atterdag, the Danish people entered into a new and uneasy phase of history ; for Atterdag, even when young, evinced a power and ambition that was to leave its mark on his country and to give the Hanseatic League an amount of warlike experience which, though it ended in their ultimate victory, cost them dear in men and money.

Valdemar hated the foreigners and especially their supremacy in trade; his *idée fixe* was " Denmark for the Danes " (to the Hanseatic League a most outrageous and unreasonable idea) and his first policy was an attempt to rid Denmark of the German trade monopolists with their unfair privileges, and to secure the prosperous Baltic trade for the Danes.

Had Valdemar not been faced with the clever and united policy of the League, backed as it was by unlimited money, he would, in all probability, have established Denmark as a great power, for he had a fine patience and tenacity ; but unfortunately he was a man without any great altruism, and this, together with a decided streak of greed, tended to mitigate against his work for Denmark.

Valdemar was ambitious, and, as in so many cases, ambition led him on to his undoing, and the undoing of his country.

He commenced his war on the Hansa by encouraging constant attacks on their merchant shipping, while at the same time he challenged their privileges in the fishing ports of Scånia, utterly ignoring all the charters which former Danish Kings had given them.

Valdemar was the despair of the Hanseatic League, for in him they found an opponent on whom their clever diplomacy was wasted, as he kept no agreement or treaty one day longer than it suited him.

There was constant diplomatic friction between the two powers, the Hansa reluctant to declare open opposition, and the King unchanging in his policy of annoyance.

But matters came to a head in 1361, when, only three months after a Hansa deputation had returned to Lübeck after vainly endeavouring to come to some agreement with the King, Valdemar collected a fleet, and sailed for the island of Gotland. Landing, he attacked Visby, whose immense riches, mostly in the hands of Hanseatic merchants, had for long aroused his cupidity.

Why Visby surrendered so easily is still a mystery; it was a well-built and fortified town, surrounded by a thick wall, but it fell into the hands of Valdemar after a short, sharp battle in which 1,800 Gotlanders perished. A rough cross marks the spot and bears the inscription: "Anti portas Visby in manibus Danorum ceciderunt Gutenses."

Legend tells that Valdemar had spent many months

in Visby the year before, when, disguised as an apprentice, he lived with a goldsmith, one of the great burghers of the city, and that Ung-Hanse's daughter had fallen in love with him. When he left he arranged a signal, on receiving which she was to open to him one of the great gates of the city of which her father held the key. One night she received the signal, then she stole the key from her father and opened the gate. No charming, gay, young apprentice entered to greet her with loving kisses, but a stern warrior at the head of steel-clad troops—and so love betrayed Visby, the rich and glorious, into the hands of Valdemar.

But when the Danes had sacked and pillaged the town and loaded their ships with the spoil of Visby, Ung-Hanse's lovely daughter did not stand triumphant on the deck by the side of her royal apprentice!

The burghers of Visby left their bitter lamenting over the loss of their riches and the shame of their beloved city ; in cold and dreadful rage they seized the girl, and took her in procession to one of the wall towers, and there they mured her up alive, to pay the penalty of her betrayal ; and the Maiden's Tower remains to this day as a witness to this story!

Setting aside legend, Valdemar sacked and pillaged Visby, and set sail for Denmark, his ships laden with magnificent jewels, with rich stuffs, and vessels of gold and silver, the heart's blood of the Hansa merchants ; but all his dreams of the power that this wealth would bring to him were never to be realized. A terrible storm arose, and the Baltic took the spoil of Visby, and Valdemar barely escaped with his life.

Many are the lovely legends of the sack of Visby.

Story tells that Valdemar took with him the two great carbuncles that had been set in the fretted rose windows of St. Nicholas Church, and that it was this sacrilege that produced the storm. The legend runs that, to this day, mariners see the great stones shining up through the Baltic waters—shining as they shone from their delicate tracery of grey stone, when they guided the rich merchant ships into the harbour of Visby.

This time Valdemar had gone too far, his action had declared him to the Hansa. Now it was a case of Valdemar or the League, there was no room round the Baltic for both of them.

With all his ambition and tenacity, Valdemar was a short-sighted man, he must have known that his action would make war inevitable, and he sadly underrated the power of the Hanseatic League.

On hearing the fatal news of the fall of Visby the first act of the League was to proscribe all Danish merchandise ; then they asked for, and obtained, the promise of alliance from Norway and Sweden.

Their next move was to call a Diet at Cologne. The League cities of Lübeck, Rostock, Stralsund, Wismar, Elbing, Thorn, Elborg, Kampden, Hardwick, and the semi-League towns of Brieg and Amsterdam, were represented—later these cities were joined by many others who contributed to the war tax. There were also present representatives from ten Allied States. At this diet the Hansa decided to make war on Valdemar, and levied a war tax of fourpence in the pound (value, not weight) on all Hansa merchandise.

Then war was formally declared on Valdemar. Fleets were organized in the Baltic and the North Sea,

and in 1362 these joined forces in the Baltic and proceeded to attack the Danish trading ports. At the
last moment the Norwegian and Swedish Kings backed
out, and sent no forces to the help of the Hansa towns.

Johann Wittemborg, burgomaster of Lübeck, was
given command of the fleet. At first all went well,
but then Wittemborg made the serious strategic error
of using his ship's forces in a land attack, whereupon
Valdemar, appearing unexpectedly, seized most of
the Hansa ships and carried them off complete with
stores.

There was nothing for Wittemborg to do but to
return, defeated, to Lübeck.

The heads of the Hanseatic League had a stern way
with failures. They cast him straight into prison,
deprived him of all civic rights and struck his name off
the rolls of the city ; then, after eleven miserable
months, he was ignominiously marched out to the
market-place, and his head was cut off by the public
executioner, with a sword which is still preserved in
Lübeck Museum.

Thus did the Hansa repay mistakes. After this
unsuccessful campaign, the Hansa were reduced to
making another treaty with Valdemar. But again the
Danish King proved himself incapable (or undesirous)
of keeping a treaty : he calmly continued his policy of
interference with German merchants.

Then he betrothed his daughter, Margaret, to
Hakon, who was the next in succession to the thrones
of Norway and Sweden, thus laying the foundation-
stone for a united Scandinavia.

This was too great a menace to escape the heads of

the Hanseatic League ; they were not slow to see the gravity of this danger to their Baltic trade.

Again they called a Diet in Cologne, in the room that was afterwards to become the famous Hansasaal. This Diet is important in that it was the first real record of the Hansa as a League, though nothing remains but the date and the name—the Cölnische Confederationsacte of 1367.

This time the League decided to fight Valdemar to the death and either win or perish. They appealed to the Emperor Charles, but he was " too busy and too far away " to give them any help. So the League went about their preparations without him.

Now, every one warned Valdemar of the serious menace of the League, and that the Cities would never rest until Denmark was crushed. Evidently these warnings had a serious effect upon Valdemar, for he suddenly fled from Denmark, leaving in his place a regent whom he authorized to make terms with the Cities.

In the meantime the Hansa calmly went on with their work ; on April the 16th their fleets met in the Sound. Then, for over a year, the League took their revenge for the sack of Visby. They pillaged and burnt the Danish towns on the Baltic and seized and destroyed all Danish trading vessels they came across ; everywhere victory met them, till in 1369 Denmark sued for peace.

The Treaty of Stralsund, drawn up by the Hanseatic League and signed by Valdemar in 1370, was one of the most amazing treaties ever dictated to a King ; and the terms were probably the most humiliating ever accepted by Royalty, especially when one realizes that they were not dictated by another sovereign, but by the mere burghers of a League of Cities.

The Hansa claimed the freedom of the Peninsula of Scånia (the rich herring district), and two-thirds of all its revenues, a free passage on all the Baltic Sea for a period of fifteen years, and, last and greatest insult, that during the whole of that time the League of Cities should have a final say in any choice of a ruler for Denmark.

Valdemar Atterdag was conquered, and humiliated to the depths.

His ambition had overruled his wisdom, and instead of fighting the Hansa with the greater unity and prosperity of his country he had provoked them to war, to the utter undoing of himself and Denmark.

In 1375 he died, shamed and broken by the League. How bitterly he must have regretted being tempted by the vast riches of Visby—riches that he never even brought home !

The Treaty of Stralsund established the Hanseatic League as a great and powerful body in Europe. Rich, feared and honoured, the League took its proper place among its fellows.

So the Hansa concluded the strange, protracted period of its birth and safely launched out on to its years of prosperity.

In 1376 Valdemar's five-year-old grandson was elected King of Norway, with his Mother to act as Regent for him, but he died, in 1387, at the age of sixteen, and his Mother was proclaimed Queen.

Margaret was a forceful personality, and her one

desire was to see a united Scandinavia. Her first move was to declare war on Albert of Sweden, claiming the Swedish crown through her late husband, Hakon of Norway, son of the deposed Magnus of Sweden.

Very naturally the Hanseatic League took the part of Albert, having no wish to see the three kingdoms united.

Stockholm, which remained loyal to Albert, was garrisoned by Germans, and during the long siege, the League countenanced, if it did not actually inaugurate, a body of privateers who constantly ran the gauntlet of the enemies' ships in order to carry food and stores up to Stockholm.

The body of men were named the Vitalian Brotherhood, generally shortened to the Victual Brothers.

After a long and tedious war the three Scandinavian countries were united in 1395 by the Union of Kalmar ; and by that time so many hardy adventurers had joined the Victual Brothers that the Hanseatic League found themselves in the awkward position of having fathered a child which had grown increasingly difficult to control.

The Victual Brothers had made their headquarters at Visby, and, little by little, their useful work of carrying food through the blockade deteriorated into daring and open piracy.

Helped as they were by the innumerable strong bands of robber Barons on the mainland, they were a constant menace to all the shipping on the Baltic, including the Hanseatic ships.

In 1398 the Grand Master of the Teutonic Knights led an attack against them, and succeeded in driving them out of Gotland, but this did little towards clearing the seas of these pirates, for they had many friends round the coasts who gave them shelter. Not only did they trouble the Hansa shipping, but it is recorded that Margaret of Sweden sent a letter to Richard II asking his leave to charter three ships of " Lyn " with which to combat the Victual Brothers and protect her trading ships.

In fact, the whole herring industry throughout the Baltic suffered at their hands, and England sent constant protests to the Hansa against this nuisance ; they estimated their losses, through the Victual Brothers, at twelve thousand livres, added to which many English merchants and sailors were burnt in the sack of Bergen by the pirates in 1392. For this England demanded justice from the Hansa—but all in vain. After various Hanseatic expeditions against the pirates, the League were reduced to asking England, Scandinavia and Flanders for help in wiping out the Victual Brothers ; but still for many years the League had no success, and lost heavily through the interference with her trade.

The two great leaders of the pirates were Godeke Mickelsen and Klas Stortebecker, both said to be noblemen of Verden, in Hanover.

Stortebecker had early taken to evil ways, and was banished after having been caught on a pillaging expedition to Hamburg. After this he joined his old friend, Godeke Mickelsen, who was the leader of the Victual Brothers ; he was eagerly received, for their ranks were largely made up of daring and dissolute young noblemen of the neighbouring provinces.

So wild and spectacular were the exploits of these

two men that their fame was soon widespread, and they passed into legend, and lived for hundreds of years in the German folk songs known as the " Stortebecker-lieder."

Their activities were by no means confined to the Baltic, for they harried the North Sea, and even sailed down as far as Spain, where they plundered a convent, and took from it some relics of St. Vincent.

When they were driven from the Baltic, Stortebecker went down to Friesland, where he married the daughter of one Keno de Broke. It is said that the gentle young girl sailed with him on all his expeditions ; if she did, she must have seen a great deal of wild life, for Stortebecker had no gentle way with his prisoners, the wealthy ones he held to ransom, the strong ones he used on his nefarious business, and the weak ones walked the plank.

Many and dreadful are the tales of the cruelty of these two leaders and their able lieutenant Wigbold, a cultured Master of Arts, who had left his books for the pleasures of piracy.

Yet in a moment of repentance, or more probably as a bid for celestial favour, they gave seven magnificent stained-glass windows to the cathedral of Verden and founded in that city a charitable bequest for providing the poor with bread.

From 1394 to 1420 the Hanseatic League were fighting the Victual Brother pirates, and it is easy to understand what it must have cost them in money for equipping expeditions and in their very considerable trade losses. One expedition alone is said to have cost Lübeck 9,350 marks.

After several small and partially successful attacks,

in none of which the leaders were captured, a fleet was equipped under the leadership of Simon of Utrecht, a Flamand resident in Hamburg. He led the expedition in his ship, one of the largest of that day, which for some unknown reason he named the " Brindled Cow "; perhaps he chose this name in bravado as Stortebecker's ship was called the " Mad Dog " !

The Hansa fleet came up with the pirates, where they lay off the coast of Heligoland. A fierce battle raged for three days, and ended in a hand-to-hand fight between Stortebecker and Simon, who had boarded the " Mad Dog." At last, though not without difficulty, the daring Klas was overpowered and cast into chains.

In triumph Simon bore him back to Hamburg, where, after vainly trying to bribe his captors to release him, he was hanged, with the rest of the captured pirates.

But Godeke Mickelsen and Wigbold were still at large, so off went Simon of Utrecht in his " Brindled Cow " again, and did not rest until he had captured the remaining pirates, who were brought to Hamburg, where they suffered the same fate as Stortebecker.

So ended the Victual Brother pirates. Encouraged in their inception by the Hanseatic League, they had lived to cost that organization all too dear, and one would have thought that the Hansa would have had a lesson in dealing with pirates ; but, though it was never actually proved, it is fairly evident that they once more made use of pirates in subduing the prosperous Norwegian trade at Bergen.

Few were the tools the Hansa would not use in gaining their longed-for monopoly. But the following excerpt from Hakluyt will prove how dearly they paid for the help of the Vitalian Brotherhood :

" William Esturmy, knight, and John Kington, Cannon of Lincolne, (being in this behalfe sufficiently authorized and deputed as Ambassadours, procurators, messengers and commissioners, by our said soverigne lord the king, namely in regard of the molestations, injuries, and damages unjustly done and committed against the liege people and subjects of the aforesaid most excellent Prince and Lord, Lord Henry by the grace of God King of England and France, and Lord of Ireland, by the communalties of the cities of Wismer and Rostok underwritten, their common council being assembled for the same purpose, and authorized also, and as well closely as expressly maintained and ratified, by the whole companie of the common society of the marchants of the Dutch Hans) doe, in this present diet at the towne of Hage situate in the countrey of Holland, being appointed for the very same occasion, demaund of you Syr John de Aa, knight, and Hermannus Meyer deputies for the cities of Wismer and Rostok, and sufficiently ordeined by authoritie requisite in this behalfe, to be the procurators and messengers of the said cities, that convenient, just and reasonable satisfaction and recompense may certainly and effectually be done unto the injured and endamaged parties, who are specified in the articles under written :—

" Imprimis, that about the feast of Easter, in the yeere of our Lord 1394, Henry van Pomeren, Godekin Michael, Clays Sheld, Hans Howfoote, Peter Hawfoote, Clays Boniface, Rainbek and many others, with them of Wismer and of Rostok, being of the society of the Hans, tooke, by maine force, a ship of Newcastle upon Tine, called Godezere sailing upon the Sea towards Prussia, being of the burthen of two

hundred tunnes, and belonging unto Roger de Thorne-
ton, Robert Gabiford, John Paulin, and Thomas de
Chester : which ship, together with the furniture
thereof amounteth unto the value of foure hundred
pounds : also the woollen cloth, the red wine, the
golde, and the sums of money contained in the said
ship amounted unto the value of 200 marks of English
money : moreover they unjustly slew John Patanson
and John Russel in the surprising of the shippe and
goods aforesaid, and there they imprisoned the sayde
parties taken, and, to their utter undoing, detayned
them in prison for the space of three whole yeeres.

" Item, that in the yeere of our Lorde 1394, certaine
persons of Wismer and Rostok, with others of the
Hans their confederates robbed one Richard Horuse
of Hull of divers goods and marchandizes in a ship
called the Shipper Berline of Prussia, being then
valued at 160 nobles.

" Item, that in the yeere of our Lorde 1395, Hans
van Wethemonkule, Clays Scheld, Godekin Mighel,
and one called Strotbeker, by force of armes, and by
assistance of the men of Wismer and Rostok, and
others of the Hans, did upon the Sea near unto Norway,
wickedly and unjustly take from John Tutteburie,
five pieces of waxe, four hundred of werke, and halfe
a last of osmundes, and other goods, to the value of
foure hundred seventie sixe nobles.

" Item in the yeere of our Lorde 1396, one John
van Derlowe, Hans van Gelder, and other their
complices of the Hans villainously and unjustly tooke
a shippe of William Terry of Hul called the Cogge,
with thirtie wollen broad clothes, and a thousand
narrow clothes, to the value of 200 pounds.

" Item in the yeere of our Lorde 1398, one John
van Derlowe, Wilmer, Hans van Gelder, Clays Sheld,
Everade Pilgrimson, and divers others of the Hans,
did upon the Sea neere unto Norway villainously and

unjustly take a shippe of John Wisedome of Hull called the Trinitie, with divers goods and marchandizes, namely oyle, waxe, and werke, to the value of 300 pounds.

" Item, in the yeere of our Lord 1399, one Clays Scheld, and others above written of Wismer and Rostok, with certaine other of the Hans, their confederates, wickedly and unjustly took from one William Pound marchant of Hull, two cakes of waxe, to the value of eighteen pounds, out of the shippe called the Hawkin Derlin of Danzig.

" Item, in the yeere of our Lord 1394, one Goddekin Mighel, Clays Scheld, Storbiker, and divers others of Wismar and Rostok, and of the Hans, wickedly and unjustly tooke out of a ship of Elbing (the master whereof was called Henry Puys) of the goods and marchandises of Henrie Wyman, John Topcliffe and Henry Lakenswyther of Yorke namely in werke, waxe, osmunds and bowstaves to the value of 1060 nobles.

" Item, in the yeere of our Lorde 1394, certaine malefactors of Wismer and Rostok, with others of the Hans, their confederats, wickedly and unjustly took out of a ship of Holland (the master whereof was called Hinkensman) 140 woollen clothes (the price of one of which clothes was eight nobles) from Thomas Thester of Yorke, and a chest, with armour, silver and golde of the aforesaid Thomas, to the value of nine pounds.

" Item, in the yeere of our Lord 1393, certaine malefactors of Wismer and Rostok, with others their complices of the Hans, wickedly and unjustly tooke from one Richard Abel of London, woollen cloth, green cloth, meale and fishes, to the value of 133 li. (vres) 6s.

" Item, in the yeere of our Lorde 1405, about the feast of S. Michael, one Nicholas Femeer of Wismer, marchant of the Hans, with the assistance of others his complices of the Hans aforesaide, wickedly and unjustly tooke from one Richard Morley, citizen of London, five lasts of herrings, besides thirty two pounds, in the sea called north Sound.

" Item, in the yeere of our Lord 1398, about the moneth of September, one Godekin Wisle, and Gerard Sleyre of Wismer and Rostok, with others of the Hans, their confederats wickedly and unjustly tooke out of a ship of Prussia (whereof the master was named Rorebek) from John Seburgh marchant of Colchester, two packs of woollen cloth to the value of an hundered marks : from Stephan Flispe, and John Plumer, marchants of the same town, two packs of woollen cloth to the value of sixty pounds : from Robert Wight marchant of the same towne, two packs of woollen cloth to the value of one hundred marks : from William Munde marchant of the same town, two fardels of woollen cloth, worth forty li(vres). And from John Dawe and Thomas Cornwaile merchants of the same town, three packs of woollen cloth worth two hundred marks, moreover they tooke and imprisoned certaine English men which were in the said ship, namely William Fubborne, servant unto John Diere, Thomas Mersh, servant unto Robert White, which Thomas paid for his ransome twenty nobles of English money, William Munde merchant of the town aforesaid, which William, by reason of the extremity of that imprisonment lost the sight of his eyes, and Thomas Cornwaile, merchant of the aforesaid towne, which Thomas paid for his ransome twentie nobles.

" Item in the yeere of our Lorde 1394, certaine malefactors of Wismer and Rostok, upon the coasts of Denmarke and Norway, beneath Scawe, and at Anold, tooke Thomas Adams and John Walters marchants of Yermouth ; and Robert Caumbrigge and Reginald Leman, marchants of Norwich, in a certaine shippe of Elbing in Prussia (whereof one Clays Goldesmith was master) with divers woollen clothes of the saide Thomas, John, Robert and Reginald, to the value of one thousande marks English, and carried the persons and goods aforesaid, away with them : and the said Thomas, John, Robert and Reginald they imprisoned at Courtbuttressow, where they detained them, untill they paide an hundred markes for their redemption.

" Item, in the yeere of our Lorde 1401, some of the inhabitants of Wismer and of Rostok, wickedly tooke at Longsound in Norway, a certaine shippe of West-Stowe in Zeland (the master whereof was one Gerard Dedissen) laden with diverse goods and marchandises of John Hughson of Yermouth, namely with the hides of oxen and of sheepe, with butter, masts, sparres, boordes, questingstones and wilde werke, to the value of an hundred marks, and do as yet detaine the said things in their possession, some of the Hans being their assistants in the premisses.

" Item, in the yeere of our Lorde 1402, certaine of the Hans of Rostok, and of Wismer, tooke upon the coast of England, neere unto Plimmouth a certaine barge called the Michael of Yarmouth (whereof Hugh ap Fen was the owner and Robert Rigweys the master) laden with bay salt, to the quantitie of 130 wayes, and with a thousand canvasse clothes of Britaine, and doe as yet detaine the saide goods in their possession, the said Hugh being endamaged, by the losse of his ship, and of his goods aforesaid 800 nobles and the forsaid Master and the mariners loosing, in regard of their wages, canvas and armour, 200 nobles.

" Item in the yeere of our Lord 1405, certaine malefactors of Wismer wickedly and unjustly tooke, in a certaine port of Norway called Selaw, a ship of Yarmouth (the owner thereof was William Oxney and the master Thomas Smith) laden with salt, cloth, and salmon, to the value of 40 pound, and doe as yet detaine the said ship and goods in their possession, some of the Hans their confederates ayding and assisting them at the same time.

"Item, in the yeere of our Lord 1395, one Godekin Mighel, Clays Scheld, Stertebeker, and other their accomplices of the Hans took upon the sea a certain ship of one John Dulwer of Cley, called the Friday (whereof Laurence Tuk of Cley was master) and conveighed the said ship unto Maustrond in Norway, and the said master and mariners they robbed of divers commodities, namely of artillery, furniture, and salt fishes being in the same ship, to the value of 500 nobles.

"Item in the yeere of our lord 1395, Godekin Mighel, Clays Scheld, Stertebeker, and other their accomplices of the Hans, unlawfully tooke upon the sea a certaine ship of one William Bets of Cley called the Margaret (wherein Robert Robines was the master) and conveyed the said ship unto Maustrond in Norway, and there robbed the said master and his partners of divers commodities, namely of artillerie, furniture, and salt fishes, to the value of 400 nobles, and one of the said masters mates they maliciously drowned.

"Item, in the yeere of our Lord 1395, about the feast of the nativitie of S. John Baptist, the forenamed Godekin and Stertebeker, with others their accomplices of the Hans, unlawfully took upon the sea a certaine ship of Nicholas Steyhard and John Letis of Cley called the Nicholas (whereof John Prest was master) and conveyed the said ship unto Mawstrond, and there robbed the said master and his companie of divers commodities, namely of furniture and salt fishes, being in the said ship, to the value of 320 nobles.

"Item, in the yeere of our Lord 1395, about the feast aforesaid, the said Godekins and Stertebeker, and their companions of the Hans unjustly took upon the sea a certaine ship of Thomas Peirs of Cley called the Isabel (whereof William Noie was master) and conveyed it unto Mawstrond, and there robbed the said master and his company of divers commodities, as namely of furniture, and salt fishes being in the said ship, to the value of 406 nobles.

" Item, in the yeere next above mentioned, upon the Saterday, about the foresaid feast, the forenamed Godekins and Stertebeker, and other their accomplices of the Hans, unlawfully took upon the sea, a certain ship of one Thomas Lyderpole of Cley, called the Helena, wherein Robert Alwey was master, and also wickedly and unjustly drowned in the bottom of the sea divers commodities, as namely salt fishes, together with the ship itselfe.

" Item, in the yeere of our Lord 1398, about the feast of St Michael the archangel, the aforesaid Godekin and Stertebeker, with other their confederats of the Hans, took at Langsound in Norway a certain crayer of one Thomas Motte of Cley, called the Peter, (wherein Thomas Smith was master) and the aforesaid crayer they wickedly and unjustly carried away, being worth 280 nobles.

" Item, in the yeere of our Lord 1395, about the feast of the nativitie of S. John the Baptist, the forenamed Godekins and Stertebeker, and others of the Hans unjustly tooke a certain ship of Simon Durham, called the Dogger-ship, and the Peter of Wiveton, laden with salt fishes, (whereof John Austen was master) upon the coast of Denmarke. And they carried away the saide Dogger, with the furniture thereof, and the aforesaid salt fishes, to the value of 170 pound. Moreover the master, and 25 mariners in the same ship they maliciously slewe, and a certaine ladde of the saide Dogger they carried with them into Wismer.

" Item, in the aforesaid yeere, and about the feast aforesaid, the forenamed Godekins and Stertebeker, with other their complices, unjustly tooke upon the

sea a certaine ship of Thomas Lyderpole, and John
Coote of Wiveton : and the master and the mariners
which were in the said shippe, they villanously slue,
among whom they put to death one Simon Andrew,
the godsonne, nephew, and servant of the aforesaid
Simon Durham. Which ship, with the goods and
furniture that were therin was worth 410 nobles.

" Item, in the very same yeere, about the feast
aforesaid, the forenamed Godekins and Stertebeker
and other their complices wickedly spoiled a certaine
ship of the foresaid Simon Durham called the Dogger,
wherein Gervase Cat was master, lying at anker, while
the companie were occupied about fishing, and likewise unjustly tooke away with them the salt fishes,
and furniture of the said ship. Moreover, the master
and his companie that were in the said Dogger, the
beate and wounded, so that they utterly lost their
fishing for that year, and the master and his said
companie being endamaged thereby, to the summe
of 200 nobles.

" Item, in the yeere of our Lord 1396, the foresaid
Godekins and Stertebeker, and other their complices
unjustly tooke upon the sea a certain crayer, called
the Buss of Zeland, which one John Ligate, marchant,
and servant unto the forenamed Simon Durham had
laden in Prussia, on the behalf of the said Simon, to
saile for England, and spoiled the said craier, and also
tooke and carried away with them the goods and
marchandises of the said Simon, being in the foresaid
ship, to the value of 66 pounds.

" Item, in the yeere of our Lord 1397, certaine malefactors of Wismar and Rostok, with certaine others of
the Hans, tooke a crayer of one Peter Cole of Zeland,
called the Busship, which Alan Barret the servant and
factor of the foresaid Simon Durham had laden with
mastes, sparres, and other marchandize, for the behalfe
of the said Simon, and unjustly tooke from thence the

goods of the said Simon, to the value of 24 pounds, and carried the same away.

" Item, in the yeere of our Lord 1394, certaine malefactors of Wismer and others of the Hans unjustly tooke upon the sea, and carried away with them a packe of woollen cloth of the foresaid Simon, worth 42 pounds, out of a certain crayer of one Thomas Fowler of Lenne being laden and bound for Dantzik in Prussia.

" Item, pitifully complaining the marchants of Lenne doe avouch, verifie and affirme, that about the feast of S. George the martyr, in the yeere of our Lord 1394, sundry malefactors and robbers of Wismer and Rostok, and others of the Hans, with a great multitude of ships, arrived at the towne of Norbern [1] in Norway, and tooke the said town by strong assault, and also wickedly and unjustly took al the marchants of Lenne there residing with their goods and cattels, and burnt their houses and mansions in the said place, and put their persons unto great ransoms : even as by the letters of safeconduct delivered unto the said marchants it may more evidently appear to the great damage and impoverishment of the marchants of Lenne : namely, Imprimis they burnt there 21 houses belonging unto the said marchants, to the value of 440 nobles.   Item, they tooke from Edmund Belyetere, Thomas Hunt, John Brandon, and from other marchants of Lenne, to the value of 1815 pounds." [2]

[1] Norbern, i.e. Bergen. (Author's note.)
[2] *The Principal Voyages of the English Nation*, Hakluyt, Vol. I, pp. 150–7. (Everyman Edition.)

BERGEN KONTOR SECRETARY'S SEAL

PART II

APOGEE OF THE HANSEATIC LEAGUE

CHAPTER VII

AFTER the fall of Visby, Lübeck was chosen as the headquarters of the Hanseatic League ; it rapidly grew to be a city of the first rank, and took a leading place in the Hanseatic war with the Victual Brother pirates.

When, in 1356, the city appealed to the Emperor Charles IV for help against Valdemar, he had refused it, but after the Treaty of Stralsund he realized that the Hanseatic League was a power to be reckoned with. Then, finding himself in a position in which some of the League funds would be useful, he sent them a notice intimating that he would be pleased to honour his Free City with a visit.

Lübeck was surprised and not too pleased, but their diplomatic sense did not fail them, and they received him with every mark of honour and respect ; although the rich burghers pulled many a wry face over the vast sums that the entertainment of Charles and his large entourage would cost the city coffers.

In October, 1375, the Emperor Charles, with his Empress and a lengthy train, entered the city of Lübeck, its first Imperial visitor since Barbarossa.

With magnificent pomp and ceremony the citizens laid themselves out to entertain their guest. Outside the walls, at the St. Gertrude Chapel, in which were preserved the relics of Thomas à Becket (which Edward III had presented to the Burgomaster of Lübeck, when he had been sent to England as the Minister of the Hansa to obtain a confirmation of their Ancient Privileges), the Emperor's train halted and arrayed themselves in their gorgeous robes of state and jewelled regalia ; there they were met by a great procession of all the leading men of the City, who escorted them through the Burghtor into the inner city.

After a High Mass, celebrated in the Cathedral, they were led in procession to the two houses in the Johannesstrasse, which had been allotted to them, the King occupying one and his Queen the other. As a mark of consideration these two houses, which were on opposite sides of the street, had been connected by a covered passage on the second floor, so that there was no need for either of the Royal personages to pass through the street if they wished to see one another.

Charles stayed ten days, and throughout the whole of the time the City provided the most brilliant entertainments.

As a proof of their signal goodwill the City invited him to a Civic Council, where the two parties exchanged civilities—equally false and fulsome on both sides !

Charles got little satisfaction out of the Hanseatic League ; they had not forgotten his refusal to help them in their hour of need, and now that they were strongly established and powerful they showed him that his favour was no longer necessary to them. They did not stint him of compliments or entertainments, and presented him with rich gifts on his departure, but that was as far as they would go ; and the League made it plain that they were not going to finance any of Charles's schemes.

So, probably burning with well-concealed rage at the failure of his plans, Charles rode out of Lübeck, passing, at the head of his train of brilliant courtiers, through the massive, grey Mulenthor, while the City burghers returned to their homes, to pull long faces and grumble at the cost of the Imperial visit ; the while rejoicing in their hearts at having reached a point where they need no longer sue for Imperial favour.

Thus Lübeck came to take its place at the head of the Hanseatic League—a place which, despite the acute rivalry of Cologne, Bremen and Hamburg, it never relinquished.

In the Rathus were held the Hansa Diets, increasing in pomp and ceremony as the power of the League grew and spread.

From the rather scanty written records it is evident that there was never any absolutely fixed rule of procedure, just as there were no fixed laws of policy. For instance, there were no settled dates for the holding of Diets—they were held when any special emergency arose—nor was there any set place, for, though Lübeck was generally chosen, several Diets were called at Cologne, while others, of which records still remain, were held at Hamburg, Wismar, Stralsund and Danzig.

One of the great stumbling-blocks to these meetings was the matter of expense, and the difficulty of travel, therefore they were generally convened round about Whitsuntide, when the roads were at their best.

Each Hansa city was called upon to send a representative ; if they failed to do so, they not only had no say in any decision that was arrived at during the session, but were liable to be fined for the first omission and, after repeated negligence, to be punished by *Verhansung*. Un-Hansing was the most severe punishment that the League meted out to merchants, cities and even countries, and it signified that they were cast out of the League and might participate in none of its privileges.

There are instances on record of merchants being un-Hansed for selling inferior goods ; and, at one time and another, various cities were un-Hansed for conduct repugnant to the heads of the organization.

In 1356 Bremen disobeyed the Hansa edict by trading with the Low Countries when they had been put out of bounds, and the city was un-Hansed for nearly thirty years, at the end of which it was faced with absolute ruin : and in 1374 Brunswick was un-Hansed for rising against its ruling powers, and after six years' misery the city sent representatives to sue for reinstatement. These unfortunate men, two burgomasters and eight citizens of note, were made to walk in procession through the streets of Lübeck barefooted, wearing long penitential gowns, and carrying candles ; arrived at the Rathus they were made to kneel and beg for the League's pardon and the favour of reinstatement—this at a fully attended Hansa Diet.

Therefore, for towns to risk un-Hansing was no light matter, yet, on the other hand, it was a very costly undertaking to attend the Diets for, apart from the expense of travelling, each representative had to be well and richly dressed, and to keep up a certain state, for the heads of the Hanseatic League were extremely particular that all honour was done to the League.

There are extant records of forty-three diets (the authorities differ about this number, but this is generally accepted as being the correct number). Dr. Walther Stein tabulates them as follows : between the years 1360 and 1400 there were twenty-four ; between 1400 and 1440 there were only twelve ; and between 1440 and 1480 there were only seven. This points to the period between 1360 and 1480 as being the apogee of the League.

The Diet of 1477, held at Lübeck, is generally cited as the one at which most towns were represented, the number being thirty-eight ; while the last Diet called in February, 1630, at Lübeck, was only attended by representatives from Lübeck, Bremen and Hamburg.

From various written records it is evident that important decisions were decided by a majority vote (the cities unrepresented having to abide by the decision), and the law used in almost all cases was " Lübeck Law," which was held in high esteem throughout Europe.

Though we have no written records of Diet procedure, we do know that every variety of subject was discussed, from complaints of bad merchandise to cases of Hanseatic merchants being ill-treated in foreign countries ; prices and tolls were fixed ; upkeep and policing of roads was arranged for ; future policy, both commercial and political, was agreed upon ; and arrangements were made for the many and expensive Hanseatic missions. For instance, at the Diet of 1604 two members each were selected from the cities of

Lübeck, Bremen, Cologne, Hamburg and Danzig, and were sent to London, under the leadership of Krefting of Bremen, to beg the King to renew their ancient privileges. James granted them an audience on August 4th, but on September 28th he " found himself in no position to renew their privileges."

More than once Kings and Queens were weighed and found wanting at the Hansa Diets, while, in more favourably considered cases, arrangements were made for receiving Crown Jewels and Regalia as security for the loan of large sums of ready money.

These Diets mark the unity and Civic status of the League. It had passed from being a mere protective league of merchants into a widespread and powerful organization of cities. One of the first Diets summoned at Lübeck in 1359 called together representatives of the " German Cities " using the formula : " Omnes Communiter ad Hansum Theutonicum pertinentes civitates."

It must never for one moment be imagined that the Hansa was a democratic body, far from it : the heads of the organization were the aristocracy of trade, they were all rich burghers, often merchant princes, who had travelled widely, and who, in addition to being astute business men, were men of brain and intelligence.

What was lacking in the Hansa was the slightest leaven of idealism—unless one considers the amassing of wealth an ideal. That was their sole aim, they would use any tool, and play off monarch against monarch, and country against country, with the most consummate skill, in order to attain their end—a trade monopoly.

This lack of ideals, together with their policy of nonreciprocity and their absolute refusal to move with the times, was the cause of their eventual downfall. During their period of power the League was far-famed, feared and honoured (as rich, clever scoundrels often are honoured), but it is safe to say that they were the most generally hated body in Europe. There could be little love for a League whose creed was monopoly and whose motto might well have been "The Hansa first ; the rest nowhere."

ANCIENT SEAL OF LÜBECK

CHAPTER VIII

ONE of the earliest, and certainly one of the most important, activities of the Hansa was the establishment of a modified Kontor on the peninsula at the south-west corner of Sweden.

This Peninsula of Scånia was the centre of the flourishing herring industry, and its fishing ports were a strange product of the times.

At other seasons a deserted waste of sand, between July 25th and September 29th it was one great, roaring fair. A movable town of booths and stalls called the Witten was set up, and that was, to all intents and purposes, the Hanseatic Kontor on Scånia.

Although their headquarters on Scånia were in few ways like the permanent Kontors at Novgorod, Bergen, Bruges and London, the League still enforced all their usual rules and regulations. During the herring season every manner of merchant came to Scånia to share the wonderful harvest of the sea. Danes, Brabançons, Frieslanders, Dutch, English ; and among all, and above all, the ubiquitous German merchants.

There the representatives of the League watched its interests, and enforced, as far as possible, their unswerving policy of Hanseatic monopoly.

The Hansa had a resident Alderman at Malmö, to

whom all disputes were referred, and who paid periodic
visits to the Witten during the season.

As usual the Hanseatic policy was to try and exclude
all strangers from participating in the trade ; and, if
they could not exclude them utterly, to make things
as difficult as possible for them. For instance, no
Hanseat was allowed to offer any help to a non-Hanseat,
nor to hire out his services to him.

After the Treaty of Stralsund the League had a strong
hold over the Danes, and as a result the latter were only
allowed one day in which to salt their catch.

While the main object of the Witten of Scània was
the catching and salting of herrings, this naturally
brought much trade in its wake ; and, during the
season, the fishing ports were thronged with merchants
offering a wonderful variety of goods for barter or sale.
There was a flourishing trade in salt ; and the Hansa
provided almost all the food consumed, as also the
not inconsiderable amount of beer drunk. Their merchants also brought cloth, linen and manufactured
goods for which they found a ready sale among the
visiting fishermen. In fact, the Germans drove a
flourishing trade all through the herring season.

It is impossible to over-estimate the importance of the
herring throughout the early days of commerce. The
fortunes of the Hanseatic League were built up on a
foundation of herrings ; a fact which they evidently
recognized, for the arms of the Schütting, the House of
the Herring Fishers in Lübeck, show three herrings
on a plain shield ; and the arms of the League itself
were half the Lübeck eagle and a dried stock-fish
surmounted by a crown.

With the removal, about 1425, of the herrings to the North Sea, off the coast of Holland, the prosperity of the Hansa began to decline, while the importance of the Netherlands increased owing to the influx of trade which followed in the wake of the herring fishery.

For many years Scånia was a bone of contention, belonging as it did sometimes to Sweden and at others to Denmark, while it was always coveted by the Hanseatic League.

It figured largely in the many political crises that rose between Sweden, Denmark and the League of Cities. In 1331, Magnus of Sweden, jealous of the flourishing trade of the German merchants in Scånia, repealed the ancient privileges of the Hansa and it took the League twelve years of diplomacy to get them back again.   The Lübeck merchants of Scånia suffered very greatly during the troubled period when Denmark, Sweden and Lübeck were fighting for the supremacy of the Baltic. In 1339, in the great Holstein rising, the King of Sweden, who espoused the cause of Holstein, took prisoner all the merchants of Lübeck and Hamburg whom he could lay hands on.   This was a serious blow to Lübeck, as that city did a large trade with the peninsula ; but the city countered by sending an expedition to Scånia during the herring season, and capturing all the Danish and Swedish ships and merchants.   Later on these were exchanged for the imprisoned Lübeckers.

Many and complicated were the Hansa disputes over Scånia, and it was only by playing off Sweden against Denmark, and Denmark against Sweden, in their inimitable manner, that the League managed to maintain their footing on the peninsula.

Among the many strange guilds and brotherhoods that sprang up in Scánia one of the most interesting, and certainly the most altruistic, was the Pious Brotherhood of Malmö. This Brotherhood undertook to bury all poor strangers who died unbefriended, with full church ceremonial of candles, masses and costly coffins. This organization doubtless did a great deal of good work, and was kept fairly busy, for there must have been many deaths, what with the hazards of fishing, the noisy jealous trade, with its constant disputes, and the enormous quantity of heady German beer that was consumed.

Apart from the Witten during the herring season, the Hansa did a certain amount of steady trade with Sweden, sufficient to warrant their keeping an Alderman in permanent residence at Malmö.

The first trading-posts in Scandinavia had been at Birka, on an island in Lake Mälar, the old Frisian settlement of about the ninth century ; and the renowned fairs in the Bohuslän district at the mouth of the Göta river. There is evidence of trade between Birka and pre-Hanseatic Visby. In later days the Hanseats enjoyed privileges in the maritime ports of Visby, Stockholm (where they had a strong footing, and which was garrisoned by Germans during the war between Margaret and Albert of Sweden), Kalmar, Söderköping, Nyköping and Åbo, and it was not till Gustav Vasa gained the throne that Sweden succeeded in shaking off the Hanseatic yoke,

CHAPTER IX

A T an early date the Germans sought for, and
obtained, special privileges in the Norwegian
town of Bergen, always the centre of a flourishing cod
and haddock trade.

In the town archives for the year 1343 there is mention of the " Mercatores de Hansa Theutonicorum."
The German merchants soon extended their privileges
there till, the union of cities having gained strength and
become the Hanseatic League, we find, in 1379, the
English making formal complaint that, while enjoying
special privileges in London, the Hansa denied them
rights of trading freely in Bergen and Scånia. This
is proof enough that there were English merchants
residing in Bergen and carrying on trade there, and that
these rivals were jealously watched by the Hansa.

Little by little the power of the Germans grew in
Bergen ; and, although the Norwegians were industrious and clever business men, the Hansa left no
stone unturned to ruin their trade. During the long
period of trouble between the Scandinavian Kings, the
League persuaded the Danish King to forbid the English to trade in that country, but their great opportunity
came in 1393, when the Victual Brother pirates sacked

Bergen, plundering it and burning down many of the buildings.

This was a sad blow to the city, but, with the help of the English merchants, they were beginning to get over it, when—and this time there is no doubt but that the Hansa countenanced the expedition, if they did not actually organize it—the city was attacked by another pirate, one Bartel Voet, in 1428. He despoiled the city, and the plunder was taken over by the Hansa, and sold, openly and shamelessly, at Hamburg.

This time Bergen was ruined, and there was nothing left for the citizens to do but to accept the Germans' offer of help, so that, in the end, they found themselves with their very land pledged to the League.

Certainly, when the League made peace with Denmark, in 1435, the Cities did agree—after a lot of discussion—to indemnify Bergen by paying them a sum of money, but even then they claimed the monopoly of trade in return ; and Bergen was too weak and shattered to withstand them.

The Germans proceeded to do everything in their power to exclude foreign merchants from Norway. First, they issued an edict that no traders should enter the country except through Bergen, where they first levied tolls on the merchandise and then bought up the best of it at their own prices ; then, in 1469, they passed a law by which no non-Hanseatic merchant might send to Bergen more than two ships a year, and even then he might not sell his cargo except wholesale, members of the Hanseatic League being given first choice in all such transactions.

Under these conditions Bergen became virtually a

German city, and for many years the League was so strong that foreign merchants protested in vain. One of the first successful attacks on the League in Norway was begun in 1488, in the reign of Henry VII. After constant complaints by English merchants that they were badly treated " by the Germans in Bergen," the King addressed a formal complaint to the heads of the Hanseatic Diet at Lübeck ; they promptly denied all responsibility, and put the blame on the Danes, but Henry knew his League and retaliated by forbidding the export of wool from England except in English bottoms ; but the good effect was merely transitory and the excellent diplomacy of the Hanseatic League soon succeeded in getting this embargo removed.

The Hanseatic Kontor at Bergen was situated on the water-front, the harbour and town being built in the form of a horseshoe. During the troubles with the Norwegians the Hansa seized the right-hand side and the dispossessed natives took refuge on the left—called the Overstrand.

This right-hand side of the horseshoe, called the Bridge, together with the Street of the Shoemakers, which joined it to the left-hand side, became the Hanseatic quarter, and there they established their Kontor.

The Bridge afforded access to the harbour and each section had its own wharf, where the vessels were moored and unloaded. The Norwegians nicknamed the Bridge " The Bridge of the Lice," because the Hanseats stuck so !

Thus the natives were shut out from the right-hand side of the town and from the harbour, which they could only reach by passing down the Street of the Shoe-

makers. There lived all the German artisans of the
" Five Professions " who had been encouraged by the
Hansa ; they were a wild and lawless mob who treated
the Norwegians with the greatest brutality and who
were shielded in all their outrages by the League.

No Norwegian was allowed to buy fish except by
passing down the Street of the Shoemakers ; then the
Hansa first levied tolls upon them, and later on closed
the street altogether to prevent them fraternizing with
the other half of the town. This so infuriated the
natives that at last, in 1445, enraged at the repeated
insults and ill-usage, a Norwegian, Olaf
Nielsen, a Lieutenant of the King, led the
people in revolt against the Germans ; the
attack failed, and the Hansa sent out a party
to hunt him down. They found him in
a convent, where he had taken refuge ; but
the holiness of the spot meant nothing to
the Germans—they set fire to it, and Olaf

GATE

Nielsen was burnt and with him a Bishop and sixteen
other folk !

It says much for the power of the League that the
King of Norway made no attempt at reprisals ; on the
contrary, he confirmed all the old Hanseatic privileges
and even went so far as to enlarge them.

In its earliest days this Kontor is generally said to
have consisted of twenty-two Gardens or Courts. This
word is derived from the Scandinavian word *gaard* or
gård,[1] meaning a farm or manor, and signifying all the

---

[1] In towns the same word was applied to the houses of merchants
together with yards or courts where they displayed their merchandise. (Author's note.)

various houses and outbuildings, with the spaces or courtyards they enclose.

As this word has been very generally used in speaking of the Bergen Kontor, I shall adopt it, but it must be realized that it is used with the meaning I have given above.

Of these twenty-two gardens, thirteen were situated in the commune of St. Marie and nine in that of St. Martin. Each garden was complete in itself, and each possessed its own special banner with its own device —such as the Unicorn of the Enhjørningen Garden.

Each garden was under the command of a Husbonde or Hausmeister, who kept order and was responsible for the behaviour of the apprentices, sailors and other ranks in his garden. The " youths " (that is, the young, non-Hanseatic members of the Kontor) were punished by thrashing ; the apprentices by fines or imprisonment.

The members of each garden lived apart in their own buildings during the summer, only fraternizing with those of the other gardens on State occasions ; but during the winter [1] they ate together in the Great Hall, or Schütting, though at separate tables, and afterwards sat round the communal fire, returning to their own buildings at a certain hour. Each garden was occupied by five " families " (of course they were all men, in all probability from the same city and all in various stages of Hansa apprenticeship). The Kontor was walled in and guarded by armed men with trained watch-dogs, who saw that no member spent the night outside.

[1] From St. Martin's Day till Lent.

The garden buildings were of wood, fairly large and all built after the same pattern. The ground floor was divided into rooms for the sale of merchandise, and the second floor was taken up by dwelling-rooms and offices, while at the back were large underground cellars and the kitchens.

There was also a vast communal hall, or Schütting, an enormous room with small windows in one end. Here were held meetings of the Kontor, banquets, and the famous Bergen Initiations.

The Hansa were extremely particular whom they allowed into their organization and every man had to serve an arduous apprenticeship before he attained to full Hanseatic status.

The qualification was at least seven years' residence in the city and by residence they meant residence and not merely rights of citizenship; and even then

TINDER-BOX

they were only allowed into the League with the full approval of the heads of the organization.

All had to put in a period of from seven to ten years, during which they had to pass through the various ranks before attaining to a position in which they might be chosen as councillors or aldermen.

There were six degrees, which, from the lowest upwards, were: Stubenjunge, Bootsjunge, Gesell (journeyman), Meister or Hausmeister, Achtzehuer and finally Alderman.

The young apprentices might be non-Hanseats, provided they were not English, Zealanders, Dutch, Brabançons, Flamands, nor from Nuremberg, nor from

" High-Germany," and always provided they were of German origin.

These young members of the Kontor might do no business for themselves, nor might they associate with the upper ranks, till they had served their term of years in the different degrees and attained to full Hansa status.

The Kontor was ruled by two Aldermen and a council of eighteen, with a secretary, who was generally a lawyer. The Aldermen were the heads of the Kontor, answerable only to the Headquarters Diet, but important decisions might be referred by the Aldermen and Council to Lübeck or the heads of the Wendish cities. Their word was law, and they had the right to punish all offenders and settle all disputes. The internal disagreements might never be taken to the courts of the land without written permission from Lübeck—Cologne was once un-Hansed for taking a dispute about Schlossgeld (a certain toll) before the Duke of Flanders.

The Council managed all outside affairs, and ruled the Germans who were resident in the Bergen Kontor— all vowed to celibacy and to keep the Kontor Law— with the utmost severity, the penalties including loss of citizenship, un-Hansing and even death itself.

The aspiring Hanseat might not leave the town during his term of probation and his upkeep was paid for by his city. He was under the absolute control of the Aldermen and for the whole of that period he must remain unmarried, and never sleep for a night outside the building ; this law was promulgated to prevent any lawful fraternization with the native women, who, as wives, might have had opportunities of finding out many a Hanseatic secret.

But this does not say that the members of the Kontor lived grave and pious lives ; far from it, in fact in one old chronicle they are referred to as " a pack of debauched merchants and their mistresses ! "

Certainly the life in the Bergen Kontor was brutal and primitive, but, if it was not the most creditable chapter in the history of the Hansa, the many records that have come down to us of this trading-post are of great interest.

Among the most striking are the accounts of the Bergen Initiations. These were a series of tests instituted to keep too many men from joining the Kontor at Bergen ; for, although ten years of celibacy under the gentle rule of the Hansa might well have been sufficient to make any man think twice before he decided to become a Hanseat,

WINDOW OF THE BEER-CELLAR

so numerous were the applications that the League invented these severe Initiations in an endeavour to keep the richer class merchants' sons out of the Kontor.

But in those days men would endure a great deal in order to attain to Hanseatic status, with all the wealth and power which it carried.

As I have said before, the times were brutal and gross in the extreme, and these Initiations provided most of the amusement to be found at the Bergen Kontor. To those who had once passed through them, the pleasure of administering the tests must have been considerable.

As late as 1599, Christian IV of Norway and Denmark visited Bergen and was present at an initiation by " smoke and water " ; it is on record that he thoroughly enjoyed it all, and that during one feast every pane of glass in the place was broken. But with the march of civilization these brutal games were suppressed.

The following were the three chief Hansa Initiations. In addition to these " The Five Professions " (among which the Shoemakers took first place) had special ordeals of their own, rougher and more brutal even than the Hanseatic Initiations, and during which the victim not infrequently died.

THE INITIATION BY SMOKE

On the morning chosen for the Initiation, the senior members of the Kontor passed, in stately procession, down the Street of the Shoemakers escorted by the members of the lower ranks. In their hands they carried buckets which they filled with scraps of leather, old horsehair and every imaginable filthy substance from the road ; this was destined to play the most important part in the Initiation. Among them were several masked figures, a buffoon, a Norwegian peasant and a countryman, who rushed among the crowd playing all manner of tricks.

On their return to the Schütting the initiation ceremony commenced. The candidate was drawn up the wide chimney and made fast ; then a great fire was lighted, made of all the material collected during the morning procession. Nauseated, stifled and half dead from the appalling stench, the victim was lowered from time to time and put through a severe questioning. Then, when almost at the end of his endurance, he was let down, carried out into the central courtyard of the Kontor and drenched with six tuns of water.

THE INITIATION BY WATER

This was generally celebrated round about Pentecost. The candidates were first given an enormous banquet ; then they were placed naked in a boat, and rowed out to sea.

Three times they were plunged beneath the water, and mercilessly thrashed every time they came up. This initiation was instituted to test the sex of the candidates, as once, in the early days of the Kontor, a woman had passed herself off as a man.

THE INITIATION BY STRIPES

The day before the ceremony one section of the senior Kontor members went in procession to the woods to cut long, supple rods ; while the remainder proceeded to the Schütting to build what was called "Paradise." This consisted of a series of draped-off compartments, each bearing the name of one of the gardens. Alongside these compartments was a broad bench, the Altar of Sacrifice, and beside it were arranged great bundles of the rods. Then the members whose duty it was to carry out the initiation —and these were chosen from among the strongest and most muscular—were sent early to bed " to sleep and get up their strength."

The next day the ceremony was inaugurated by a solemn procession. To the beating of drums the members of the Kontor marched out to a copse near the Bridge. They were led by the two youngest Haus-meister, who were responsible for the whole organiza-tion, and who wore masks, long black mantles and carried swords.

The procession returned to the Schütting, each member carrying a leafy branch; they then drank a glass of wine and separated, to their own quarters. After a short rest they returned to the Schütting, where the initiates had to listen to an address by one of the oldest members. He exhorted them to be orderly, diligent and faithful and warned them against drunken-ness and debauchery. He told them of the severity of the test and advised the timid to withdraw; at which they protested lustily.

At midday a great banquet was held at which the two Hausmeister presided amidst much song and merriment. While this was going on, the buffoons and clowns enlivened the company with their jests.

In the meantime the apprentices had been given a banquet, where the drinks had been plentiful. Then, one by one the victims were brought up, each more or less drunk. They were stretched out on the fatal bench, while the strongest members of the Kontor stood over them with the supple green rods; then, to the clash of cymbals, the cruel beating began. The cessation of the cymbals was a sign for a new victim to take his turn on the altar.

So dreadful were these beatings that more than one victim succumbed under them. One apprentice, Hufanos by name, sent back to his mother his blood-soaked shirt, to be shown to his friends at home.

When all the Initiations were over a discourse on the might and glory of the Kontor was given by Harlequin. The day ended with another banquet at which the initiates took part ; if they fainted from pain and fell off the benches they were beaten again, and if this failed to arouse them to an interest in the proceedings they were taken out and ducked.

The Games of the Five Professions were mostly too coarse and brutal for publication, but among them were the Stavelspiel, in which the victim was plunged in a ditch six to nine feet deep filled with lime where he had to stop for a certain time ; if he attempted to come out, he was stoned to death. The Preckespiel took place on Easter Sunday. All the German merchants went out to the St. Margaret's Cemetery, and there, one by one, the initiates had to climb to the top of the highest trees and shout out the names of all the women of ill-fame in the city, describing in the minutest detail their recent adventures with them. The Five Professions were much looked down on by the merchants and there was no fraternization between the two classes.[1]

A in most of its kontors the members of the Hanseatic League in Bergen attended one church, which, little by little, came to be regarded as their own. In Bergen it was the Maria Kirke, built in 1188, and called by the Hanseats, Vor fru Kirke. The various ranks had their own pews, the aldermen and senior members each his richly decorated stall, while, at the back of the church, a part was set aside for the " Youths."

[1] For this information I am indebted to Emile Worms, *Histoire Commerciale de la Ligue Hanséatique.* Paris, 1864.

During the period of its prosperity the members of the League made costly and beautiful gifts to the church ; the altar shone with many branched candlesticks holding candles of the finest beeswax, and the walls were decorated with paintings, for the most part Biblical subjects, but interspersed with portraits of the Hansa aldermen and priests and with long rows of shields bearing the arms of the League and Kontor,

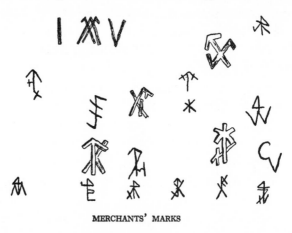

MERCHANTS' MARKS

and inscribed with the names of the donors, their devices and merchants' marks.

The Kontor members attended church in all their usual state, dressed in costly robes of fur, while at the head of each garden marched the Journeyman carrying the elaborate brass lantern of ceremony. In each country the League made a great show of the outward ceremonies of religion, though they were not above changing the form to suit the taste of the ruling monarch.

In addition to the Maria Kirke, the League were

closely associated with St. Martin's Church and with two Poor Houses, those of St. Martin and St. Catherina. The Hanseatic League took an active interest in the provision of Poor Houses and Hospitals and even Schools for the members of their organization.

In the Hanseatic Museum at Bergen there are detailed records of the later history of the following Kontors : Finnegaarden, Dramshusen, Bratten, Leppen, Revelsgaarden, Solegaarden, Kjømandsstuen, Kappen, Holmedalen, Belgaarden and Jakobsfjorden, Svensgaarden, Enhjørningen (The Unicorn), Bredsgaarden, Bugaarden, Engelsgaarden, Sostergaarden, Goldskoengaarden.

These Kontors persisted long after the Hanseatic League lost its monopoly in Bergen ; and, while the post in Bergen could no longer be called a Hanseatic Kontor in the true sense of the name, there was still a close trade with Hamburg, Bremen and Lübeck till the nineteenth century.

The following is a detailed description of THE LANTERN one Garden of the Kontor : THAT WAS CARRIED AT HANSEATIC On the ground floor was the small room, FUNERALS from which the stairs led up to the first story ; its walls were painted red or yellow, and from the beams hung the great lantern, which was lighted and placed over the entrance on all festive occasions, and carried by the Journeyman at the head of the procession of Kontor members when a Hanseat was buried in the Maria Kirke. There, too, were kept the fire-buckets, the great water-barrel—*de water tunnen*—and

BALANCE

the fire-hooks. The rest of the ground floor was taken up by a large store-room.

The first floor consisted of an outer room, a prin-cipal room and an inner room.

In the outer room, the lower ranks of the Kontor cooked their meals and spent their free time during the summer ; and there were kept the weighing scales, yard measures, keys, etc., used in the daily business. In one corner stood a food cupboard, and beneath it a large cask of ale ; against one wall stood a wash-hand basin, with a can of water suspended above it, and a roller-towel adjacent. In the window stood a heavy wooden table and bench ; while from the ceiling hung the single and double train-oil lamps, the primitive fire-pump and the grotesque stuffed fishes which were the mascots of the Kon-

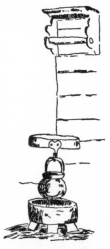

WASH-HAND STAND
AND ROLLER-TOWEL
FITMENT

tor. Whenever a " king-cod " was taken at the fish-eries, it was stuffed, and presented to the Kontor. The customers who came to do business with the merchant were first shown into this room.

From the outer room a door led into the " principal room," which was the living-room of the merchant after business hours, and the central meeting-place of the life of the garden. One corner of the room was partitioned off, and the space thus formed was the private office containing a stool and desk, with ink-stand, sand-box, and candlestick—the latter often made from an eagle's claw, if the merchant were an ardent sportsman. Through a small window in the office, the merchant could inspect the waiting client, or keep an eye on the apprentices.

SINGLE OIL-LAMP

Another feature of this room, and one that throws an interesting light on the life in the Kontor, was the " wine-cupboard." This was a large cupboard running from floor to ceiling and with double doors. Open the one door and you were confronted with ordered rows of bottles, open the other and you disclosed a secret staircase !

DOUBLE OIL-LAMP

The members of the Kontor were certainly sworn to celibacy for their term of residence, but this does not say that they were not ordinary men, and without the secret staircase many a one would have been placed in an awkward predicament if an alderman or senior member had paid them a surprise visit after business hours, when they happened to be entertaining a lady friend.

As it was, they just opened the double door of the

wine-cupboard—the visitor vanished—and they proceeded to offer their unwelcome guest a drink from the
well-stocked shelves behind the other door.

Beyond this room was another and smaller one, " the
inner room." It was divided into two ; on the one side
was the merchant's built-in winter bed, placed immediately over the stove, and with a door above it in
the outer wall,—
through which
the bed could
be made by the
female servant,
as no woman

KING-COD MASCOT

was allowed to enter the building. The other half was
furnished as a small kitchen. Here the merchant's
cooking was done during the busy summer season,
when the harbour outside the Kontor was filled with
a constantly changing fleet of fishing vessels, bringing
a rich harvest to the Hanseatic League. In winter his
cooking was done in the big Schütting, the general
club-room of the Kontor.

But the dimensions of the door above the
bed and the secret staircase both tell the
same old story, and point to the frail human-   CANDLESTICK
ity of even Hanseatic Kontor members !

On the second floor there were three rooms : the
Merchant's summer bedroom, the Journeyman's room,
and the room in which the lower ranks slept.

The Journeyman, standing immediately below the
Merchant in rank, had a room of his own ; and the
equipment of this room shows that he was a man of
authority. He kept the books, and oversaw the work

of the apprentices, to whom he also dealt out the punishments awarded by the alderman—vide the whip hanging on the wall. He also had his own desk in the principal room, and hanging above this desk there was often a typical Hanseatic motto :

" Aufrichtig sey zur jeder Zeit—
    nimme auch in Acht die Wachsamkeit."

Which one is tempted to doubt that he always lived up to. On the wall hung his testimonials, framed and

KONTOR WHIP

glazed, and often, if he had been a successful sportsman, a stuffed eagle. It was the Journeyman who bore the elaborate brass lantern at the head of a funeral procession.

The principal rooms were brightly limewashed in reds, greens and yellows, with flowing designs. The ceilings were white and the beams red painted.

The bareness of the third room testifies to the hard life lived by the lower ranks in the Hanseatic Kontor. There was practically no furniture—a bench and table, a wash-hand basin, jug and roller-towel and

COAT-
HANGER

some pegs for clothes. The beds were the usual built-in wall-beds provided with doors that could be shut in winter ; for even in the most bitter weather there was no means of heating this room.

These rooms, with their simple furniture, their weights and measures, account-books, shelves full of rolls of stuff and samples of merchandise, their wall-beds, wine-cupboards and secret staircases, were the surroundings in which the members of the Bergen Kontor passed the wearisome ten years of celibacy that was to end in all the glory of full Hanseatic status and open for them the doors of world trade, prosperity and riches.[1]

[1] For these details of life in the Bergen Kontor I am indebted to Herr Koren-Wiberg . . . *Det Tyske Kontor I Bergen*, 1899.

BERGEN KONTOR SEAL

CHAPTER X

THE HANSA IN RUSSIA

THE Hanseatic League were quick to realize the vast natural resources of Russia, and also the strategic position of Novgorod, situated on the Volkhov river, near Lake Ilmen, easily reached from the Baltic by the Neva, and on the direct trade route from the East.

As early as the eleventh century we hear of German merchants in Novgorod, while the Hanseatic merchants were accorded special privileges for their Kontor of St. Petershof in 1269. As a result of these privileges the German merchants were able to exclude almost all rival foreign merchants from this rich trading centre. To a certain extent they succeeded, and for many years the trade in Novgorod was almost exclusively in the hands of German merchants, no foreigners being allowed into the city under penalty of severe punishment. A state of affairs which led to much dissatisfaction on the part of English and European merchants.

The clever Lombard bankers who had early penetrated into Russia were intensely disliked by the Hansa, who, in 1346, after much League diplomacy, succeeded in having an interdict passed proscribing the Lombards from doing business in Russia on the grounds that they were unscrupulous and dishonest.

Once established in Novgorod the Hansa selected its site and built the great church of St. Peter's, round which were clustered the various buildings, storehouses, offices and dwelling-quarters which constituted the St. Petershof, the Hanseatic Kontor in Novgorod.

Here, as in Bergen, Bruges and London, the members were subject to Kontor laws, the principal being a residence of from eight to ten years, strict celibacy, and implicit obedience while passing through the various stages which led to full Hanseatic status.

The visiting merchants arrived in two bands, one in the spring and one in the autumn, and were called the summer and winter travellers. They resided in the Kontor and had to conform to the Kontor laws. St. Petershof was governed by one Alderman and a council of four. Here, as at Bergen, the Alderman was the only member who received a fixed wage; but at Novgorod the priest in charge of St. Peter's Church, and the priests who travelled with the summer and winter travellers, were supported by the Hansa organization, and were accorded the full dignity of Aldermen.

From the organization it is evident that the body of resident members at St. Petershof was far smaller than those at Bergen, Bruges or London; and that its numbers were largely made up of the travelling merchants.

Life in the Novgorod Kontor was lived in common rooms, some set aside for the use of the younger members of the organization, with rules slightly relaxed in their favour—as they were relaxed in favour of the winter travellers, who had to spend so many months in Russia.

This Kontor was entirely self-supporting, brewing its own beer, baking its own bread, preparing the furs and melting down the tallow and wax brought in by the Russians. In fact, living a life apart in the midst of the none too friendly natives.

These latter were treated with extreme brutality by the Hanseats, in fact the accounts of constant trouble prove that here, as in Bergen, there was little love lost between the two parties.

For instance, in the case of a man becoming insolvent, the Germans claimed first payment, taking precedence of all other creditors, even if their debts were of no long standing. The Hansa arrogance in Novgorod was notorious throughout the world; their motto was, "Who can prevail against God and the great Novgorod," but it ought to have been, " God, the Hansa, and the great Novgorod ! "

Many were the assaults made on the Hanseats, and more than once the Russians seized merchants and threw them into prison or thrashed them soundly. Then the League threatened to withdraw from Novgorod, a proceeding which would have done far more harm to the League than it would have to the Russians. As a matter of fact they did withdraw from Novgorod once or twice, but their cupidity very soon took them back again despite all their sufferings and discomfort.

In the early days of the League the Kontor at Novgorod was under the Headquarters law of Visby. In 1361, when there had been grave trouble between the German merchants and the Russians in Novgorod, Visby sent an Alderman, together with Johann Perseval of Lübeck, to look into the matter. They came to a satisfactory arrangement, and passed the important ruling that for the future the Kontor was to make no alteration in the law without first submitting it to the Cities—Visby, Lübeck, Riga, Reval and Dorpat.

After the sack of Visby by Valdemar, Lübeck saw a chance of making herself the head of the Hanseatic League, and for some years she tried to overset the claims of Visby, and to enforce Lübeck law in Novgorod. At last, in 1373, Lübeck was proclaimed the court for all Novgorod appeals, and her law was enforced in the St. Petershof Kontor.

This was the work of the famous Hanseatic diplomat, Jakob Pleskow, Burgomaster of Lübeck, and one of the cleverest and wisest men who ever ruled the Hansa.

That was the end of Visby as a great Hanseatic city ; had her law been maintained in Russia, Visby would certainly have been rebuilt and retained her position at the head of the League.

So for many years the Germans enjoyed a very rich monopoly in Russia, with their headquarters at Novgorod and with certain privileges in Pleskov and Moscow.

They bought up the natural products of the country, furs, honey, wax, skins, leather and timber, and in exchange for them gave cloth and linen from England, Flanders and Germany, and such manufactured goods as they imported. They also did a very flourishing trade in the rich Oriental merchandise so beloved by the Tartar princes, who lived in great barbaric state.

Strange indeed must their life have been up in that wild, uncivilized country. There the members of the Kontor lived, shut up in their own quarter, forbidden under penalty of death to fraternize with the natives and always under the strict rule and watchful eye of their ruling Alderman.

Yet what romance must have haunted those narrow rooms. There the winter travellers sojourned during the long dark months. They were much travelled men, men who had seen life in many other countries, they had probably lived in Visby, Bruges, Bergen, London and Venice ; so there must have been many an adventurous tale told when the long tables in the common room were cleared, the fire piled high with logs and the great Hansa pewters of beer started upon their rounds, while outside the Kontor walls the Russians lived their uncivilized lives, and grew to hate the haughty, domineering German merchants, whom they cheated whenever possible.

What wealth Novgorod must have had to offer these merchants to induce them to support these weary months of monotony and danger !

But Novgorod was not always to remain a Hanseatic monopoly. Apart from the ever-recurring disputes between the Germans and the Russians, graver issues arose. The union of Poland and Lithuania in 1386 did much to hinder the overland trade of the League ; and the serious fighting, when Prussia rose against the Order of Teutonic Knights, ending in the ceding of West Prussia to Poland in 1460, with the resultant freedom of the Vistula cities, shook the security of the Hanseatic League to its foundations.

It speaks well for the strong position of the League that it managed to weather the storm.

A still more threatening menace to the Hansa trade with Russia was the attitude of the overlords of Moscow. Novgorod was a wealthy city in early mediæval times. It was founded by Slavs, and as early as the ninth century it ruled the other settlements round Lake Ilmen. Although its trade was largely dependent on Kief, it possessed its own charter of government and was a Free City.

For many years the rulers of Moscow had turned jealous eyes towards the riches and prosperity of Novgorod. In 1332, Novgorod repulsed an attack by the rulers of Moscow; and for many years the Germans and Swedes, who were interested in the christianization of the country, gave it some semblance of protection, but under Ivan III the Russians waged constant war on the city, and in 1478 his victorious army entered Novgorod. He seized many of the citizens and carried them to Moscow, intending to replace them by his own subjects, and, in addition to this, he repealed the city charter.

This was a great blow to the Hanseatic League and a grave check to their trade; but worse still was to follow in the person of the Czar Ivan IV. He utterly subdued the city, he sacked the churches, monasteries and public buildings and killed many of the inhabitants. The most important Hanseatic merchants he took prisoner and their merchandise he confiscated.

No Hansa privileges carried any weight with Ivan

the Terrible; he not only ignored their complaints but he refused to render up his prisoners, and it was many years before the League diplomacy obtained their release; the merchandise was lost to them for ever.

This was the end of the Hanseatic Kontor in Novgorod and the end, too, of their prosperous monopoly in Russia.

In vain did Lübeck try to regain the privileges in Novgorod; for twenty years the Germans were shut out of Russia.

During the reign of Ivan's son, they were permitted to return to the city, but no longer was there any question of a German monopoly.

Foreign merchants were firmly established, and, most severe blow of all, the English had opened up a route to Russia via the White Sea and Archangel, thus obviating the necessity of the Germans as middle-men.

The Kontor at Novgorod was empty and deserted and the day of the Hansa merchants was passed.

For a time they continued to do some trade with Russia and removed what remained of their Kontor to Narva. In 1586 Czar Feodor Ivanovitch even granted them special privileges in Narva and Pleskov; but the trade was desultory and unsatisfactory, and the League never recovered from the blow dealt it by Ivan the Terrible.

St. Petershof was one of the earliest of the Hanseatic Kontors, and at its prime was one of the busiest and most prosperous; but it was the first to succumb to changing conditions.

CHAPTER XI

FLANDERS, populated by a gifted and industrious type of craftsman, possessing excellent ports and water-ways, and many well-advanced cities, offered ideal conditions for trading, and was eagerly sought by the League as a centre for the disposal of their Northern produce, and as a market in which to buy the excellent wares of the country.

According to their wont, they asked for and obtained special privileges for their big Kontor at Bruges.

In Bruges there could be no question of such a Kontor as those at Bergen and Novgorod. The city was one of the most civilized in Europe, possessed of an advanced art and culture, and rich, even in comparison to the rich Hanseatic cities.

The first treaty between Bruges and the German merchants was made in 1252 ; and by 1310 Bruges was celebrated far and wide for its flourishing trade.

In Flanders the Hanseats had to adapt themselves to the land they lived in, and control their love for the rough, brutal punishments and amusements that enlivened the northern Kontors.

The Bruges depot was the second largest of the Hanseatic Kontors ; and was governed by six aldermen and a council of twenty-eight. Although the life was more civilized, the discipline was just as rigid, and the usual rules of Kontor life—celibacy, period of probation and non-fraternization—were strictly maintained.

Bruges was the chief " School " for the upper ranks of Hanseatic merchants ; there they were trained in the manners and methods of trade, and in the subtleties of Hanseatic diplomacy ; and the punishments for any signs of individualism were extremely severe.

There seems to have been no special Kontor building in Bruges, like the ones at Bergen, Novgorod and London, but the members of the Kontor, and the agents buying and selling for the non-resident Hanseatic merchants, lived in several buildings, while the documents and seals were kept in the Reventer, the refectory of the Carmelite Monastery.

The members of the Kontor were divided into three sections. In the first were Swedes, Livonians and Gotlanders, in the second Prussians and Westphalians, and in the third Wends, Saxons and the rest.

Each of these sections was again subdivided into two, and each of the six divisions was represented by its own alderman, and by its own councillors.

The aldermen retired yearly, at Whitsuntide, when the new aldermen were installed with due pomp and ceremony, and the new councillors took their oath of obedience.

These men ruled the Kontor and managed all the complicated business transactions of the League in

Flanders ; and their post was no sinecure, for the
history of the Hanseatic League in Flanders is an
unending series of disputes and quarrels.

Here, as in the other Kontors, the revenue was
obtained from tolls and fines, and every city represented had to pay a certain amount towards the general
funds. The penalty for failing to do so was un-
Hansing, and once Cologne—always rather an unruly
member of the League, and torn by jealousy for
Lübeck—was un-Hansed for refusing to pay its dues
to the Kontor at Bruges.

The Hanseatic charter was displayed in an *arche
sainte*, called the *l'arche de Noé*, in the Sacristy of the
Carmelite Church. At that time there was no strict
line drawn between religious and secular matters,
though, to our mind, the last place one would expect
to find the Charter of the Honourable Company of
Fishsalters would be in the Sacristy of St. Paul's.

Varied indeed was the trade of Bruges, and great
was the wealth of that city, where the burghers'
wives vied with Royalty in the magnificence of their
attire and the luxury of their homes.

At one time no less than seventy trade guilds
flourished in Bruges, and representatives of every
nation were to be met with at the great fairs which
took place at intervals throughout the year. It was
there that the Hanseatic agents collected the merchandise from Flanders, Spain and England for
dispatch to their Northern centres. In Bruges, a
more advanced city than either Lübeck, Bremen or
Hamburg, there was no possibility of the League
imposing a total monopoly, but they did their best in

this direction, and, having obtained very considerable privileges, they proceeded to a policy of boycott.

At the least hint of rivalry on the part of the Flemish merchants the Hansa threatened to leave the city, and this they did on two or three occasions.

As the League brought a vast trade to the country, the citizens of Bruges were very loath to see themselves cut off from the Hansa; and in each case they ended by capitulating.

Thus, in 1388, after serious trouble between the Flemings and the Hanseats, the former resenting their autocratic methods, the League formally removed from Bruges to Dordrecht, in Holland. Then they proceeded to put Flanders out of bounds and forbid all trade with Flemish merchants. This did an immense amount of damage to the trade of the whole country, and to Bruges in particular; so, in 1391, the cities of Bruges, Ghent and Ypres sent representatives to a Hansa Diet to ask for reinstatement.

In 1392, Heinrich Westhoff, of Lübeck, managed to adjust the matter and, after Bruges had paid an indemnity of fifty thousand Lübeck marks, and the rich burghers of the city had been submitted to the usual indignities and humbled to the dust, he led the Hanseats back to their old quarters in Bruges with a pomp and magnificence which was always to the fore when the Hansa entered any city, either as autocratic monopolists or as magnanimous and forgiving magnates.

Again in 1430, annoyed by the attitude of Spain, the League boycotted Spanish wool; this made a great difference to the trade of Bruges, for much

Spanish wool was used in the cloth manufactory throughout Flanders, and the citizens did everything in their power to prevail upon the Hansa to withdraw their embargo, but all in vain. For thirteen years the League were adamant, and only relented when Spain gave in and accorded them special and valuable privileges. Finally, in 1451, the League again left Bruges and once more the whole of Flanders was put out of bounds for six years, till Bruges capitulated and again the Hansa returned in triumph.

It was during this embargo that Bremen was hardy enough to continue its trade with Flanders, upon which the League un-Hansed the city, and practically ruined it.

Such was the troubled history of the Hanseatic League in Flanders ; but, until the decline of the Hansa, the League always had the best of all quarrels with the Flemings. So great was their power and influence that even the rich city of Bruges could not get on without them.

During the various wars and internal revolutions of the Netherlands, the Hanseatic League did not suffer as much as might have been expected—only inasmuch as trade in general was very greatly hindered.

With their ever famous diplomacy they protested their absolute neutrality, and so benefited from whichever side won ; they also developed a very clever system of playing off one ruler against the other, in all of which transactions a considerable amount of profit accrued to the League. The end of Bruges as a great trading centre came through their rash policy towards Maximilian of Austria. He was a German

prince, and essentially noxious to the free Flemings ;
in a rash moment they seized him and shut him up in
the Château de Bruges, where they kept him a prisoner
for nearly six months.

It was a rash moment when they imprisoned him ;
but it was a still rasher one in which they let him go,
for he naturally proceeded to take his revenge upon
the city.

Through the Bruges Kontor the Hansa did a certain
amount of trade with France, but few records remain
to us of Hanseatic dealings with that country.

France had little to offer to the merchants of the
League ; its manufactures were negligible and its
natural products inconsiderable.   There was no Kontor
anywhere in France, but there are records of certain
French Kings granting them special privileges.

In 1294, Philippe le Bel granted to the citizens of
Lübeck, Gotland, Riga, Campden, Hamburg, Wismar,
Rostock, Stralsund, Elbing, and to all navigators in
the German Ocean, commercial liberty throughout all
his realm, on condition they never imported into
France any wool, leather or other article of English
origin.

During the long period of the French wars Charles
VII issued an edict for the capture of all Hanseatic
trading vessels ; and in 1604 there is a record of
Krefting's Hansa embassy visiting France to ask
Henri IV to renew their privileges, which had recently
been rescinded.   This was granted, and for a short
time the privileges were maintained.

The closest relations with France were those with
Bremen, Hamburg and Lübeck prior to 1810, when

these cities—the last remnants of the once powerful
Hanseatic League—rendered a certain amount of
unwilling help to France in the Napoleonic wars;
but as regards a trade history the Hansa had practically
none in that country.

Neither are there many records of trade with Spain.
Certainly Spanish wool entered the Hanseatic Kontor
at Bruges, where it was once the subject of a big
embargo; also in 1383 there is a record of King John
of Castile interdicting the Hanseatic merchants within
his realm; which interdict was lifted in 1472.

In 1552, Philip II made a treaty with the Hansa
in which he gave them various privileges; evidently
these privileges were not kept; for in 1604 Krefting's
embassy approached the Spanish rulers in Brussels
with a request that they would remove the crippling
tax they had levied on various Hanseatic merchandise.

Certainly Spain considered the Hanseatic League a
power in the land, for in 1627, when the might of the
Hanseatic League was practically at an end, the King
of Spain sent a delegate to a Hanseatic Diet at Lübeck,
with proposals for an alliance between the League and
Spain; but by that time the League was well past its
prime and nearing the time when it was a name and
nothing else.

In Portugal the League had an agency at Lisbon,
and did a prosperous trade, but this mainly passed
through the confederation of South German cities,
Ulm, Nuremberg and Augsburg, which cities, although
affiliated to the League, were never an integral part
of it.

Through these same cities the Hanseatic League

carried on a big trade with Venice, where they had a modified Kontor in the Fondago di Tedeschi on the Grand Canal, where they handled all their rich Italian trade, but this was never a Kontor in the true sense of the word.

In Venice the autocratic and high-handed Hanseats took a second place, and were always in subjection to the Italians. This building, with its living quarters, storehouses and shops, was only open to the members of the Hansa at certain periods of the year, and they might only reside there for a stated time. While in the Fondago, the Hanseats were under the rule of a resident Italian secretary, who weighed, measured and inspected all goods bought and sold and who audited all accounts. Their trade, too, was confined to the Venetians only, and the Venetian authorities had the final say in all business matters.

It is extraordinary that the Hanseatic League, usually so haughty and overbearing in all trade relations, put up with this treatment, and did not remove from Venice ; but for some reason or other they not only put up with it but evidently liked it, for positions in the Venice agency were in great demand amongst the merchants, and there is plenty of evidence that the Germans and Venetians got along together extremely well, for in 1508 the Venetians made a successful appeal to the Hanseatic League for help against their aggressors—the Kings of France and Spain and the Pope.

These were the relations of the Hanseatic League with the South European countries from the thirteenth century onwards, and all the evidence points to the fact that the main Hanseatic trade with Southern Europe passed through the Bruges Kontor, and that their business with France, Spain and Portugal was a minor consideration.

LÜBECK-BERGEN SAILOR'S SEAL

CHAPTER XII

IN England the Hanseatic League was already provided with an excellent foundation on which to build up their cherished system of monopoly. There is evidence that, from the earliest days of the leagues of cities, German merchants had carried on a trade with England. Thorpe in his *Ancient Laws and Institutions* states that, in *De Institute Londonie of Ethelred*, 988–1016, the German merchants are referred to not by the names of their cities, but as " Homnies Imperatoras qui Veniebunt in Navibus suis," and that not only Germans but Flemish guilds of cities were recognized by the King.

Realizing the success of these early traders, the League was anxious to establish friendly relations with the English ruling powers, and, once the guilds of cities were united under the Hansa, the League, with its rapid increase in power and wealth, were able to ensure privileges and charters by making themselves indispensable to the English kings.

The first important charter granted to the German merchants was that between Henry II and the Emperor Barbarossa in the early days before the cities were united under the Hansa ; and this was followed in 1194 by very special privileges granted to " Zie Cölner " by Richard Cœur de Lion.

In the hour of his need the city of Cologne had received the King with great friendliness, and had contributed large sums of money towards paying off his ransom. In return, he exempted them from the payment of any rent for their " Gildhalle " in Thames Street, and granted them special privileges for buying and selling throughout his realm.

These privileges granted to the German merchants were the basis of the power and prosperity of the Hanseatic League, and were continually being confirmed and repealed and reconfirmed by successive English kings up to the time of Elizabeth.

In the early period it was not only German merchants who visited England. The Flemings came in search of raw wool, produced to such a degree of excellence in England, but at that time hardly worked at all in this country. This wool was carried to Flanders in German bottoms, where it was worked and exported to all the European countries. No small amount of it was brought back to England by the German merchants and sold at a large profit.

In 1199 King John issued a safe-conduct to all foreign merchants :

" A generall safe conduct graunted to all forreine Marchants by King John in the first yeere of his reigne, as appeareth in the Records of the Tower, Anno 1, Regis Joannis.

" John by the grace of God etc., to the Maior and the communaltie of London, Greeting. You are to understand, that it is our pleasure, that all Marchants, of what nation soever, shall have safe conduct to passe and repasse with their marchandize into England. It is our will also, that they be vouchsafed the same favour in England, that is granted unto the English Marchants in those places from whence they come. And therefore we give you in charge, that you cause this to be published, and proclaimed in your baili-wicke, and firmely to be observed, permitting them to goe and come, without impediment, according to the due, right and ancient customes used in your said Bailiwicke. Witnesse Geofry Fitz-Peter, Earle of Essex, at Kinefard, the 5 day of April.

"The same forme of writing was sent to the Sherife of Sudsex, to the Maior and communaltie of the Citie of Winchester, to the Baily of Southampton, the Baily of Lenne, the Baily of Kent, the Sherife of Norfolke and Sufolke, the Sherife of Dorset and Sommerset, the Barons of the Cinque-Ports, the Sherife of South-amptonshire, the Sherife of Hertford and Essex, the Sherife of Cornewal and Devon." [1]

In the reign of Henry III there was a long corre-spondence between the King and Haquinus of Norway concerning the mutual treatment of merchants in the respective countries. Both rulers were willing to allow merchants free entrance to their countries and every facility for trade whilst resident there.

An interesting point appears in the following excerpt from a letter of Henry :

"A mandate for the King of Norway his Ship called the Cog.

"Wee will and commaund all bailifes of Portes at the which the Cog of Norway (wherein certaine of the King of Norwaie his soldiers and certaine marchants

---

[1] *The Principal Voyages of the English Nation*, Hakluyt, Vol. I, p. 109. (Everyman Edition.)

of Saxonie are coming for England) shall touch, that, when the foresaid Cog shall chance to arrive at any of their Havens, they doe permit the said Cog safely to remaine in their said Havens so long as neede shall require, and without impediment also freely to depart thence, whensoever the governours of the sayd ship shall thinke it expedient. Witnesse the King." [1]

From the above letter it is evident that the German merchants were quick to avail themselves of any ships —even Norwegian ones—that were privileged to enter English ports.

In 1236 Henry III confirmed all the privileges granted by Richard I to the Cologne merchants; exempting them from the payment of

" those two shillings which they were wont to pay out of their Guildhall in London or in any other place in our dominions : and that they may safely resort unto Fayers throughout our whole kingdome, and buy and sell in the citie of London." [2]

The King also granted a seven years' charter to the city of Lübeck,

" at the earnest request of our trusty brother Richard, Earle of Cornewal, being of late elected King of the Romanes, . . . provided that the sayd burghers doe in the meanetime behave themselves well and faithfully towards the foresaid elected brother." [3]

On the above conditions the merchants of Lübeck were granted safe-conduct in England, permission to buy and sell, and immunity from all seizure and con-

---

[1] *The Principal Voyages of the English Nation*, Hakluyt, Vol. I, p. 110. (Everyman Edition.)
[2] Ibid., Vol. I, p. 110.   [3] Ibid., Vol. I, p. 111.

fiscation or other form of molestation.   This mandate was repeated to the burghers of Brunswick, and the merchants of Denmark.

In 1260 Henry granted a charter to the " Marchants of Almaine " as shown by the following excerpt :

" A charter for the Merchants of Almaine, who have an house at London commonly called the Guild Hall of the Dutch, graunted in the 44 yeere of Henry the third, renued and confirmed in the 1 and 29 yeere of Edward the first.

" At the request of the most gracious Prince Richard king of the Romanes our most deare brother, wee doe graunt unto the Marchants of Alemain (namely unto those that have an house in our citie of London, commonly called the Guildhall of the Dutch Merchants) that we will, Throughout our whole Realme, maintaine all and every of them, in all those liberties and free customes, which both in our times, and in the times of our progenitors, they have used and enjoyed.   Neither will we enforce them beyond these liberties and free customes, nor in any wise permit them to be inforced.   In witnesse whereof, wee have caused these our letters to be made patents." [1]

During the reign of Edward I there was issued an important mandate—the Carta Mercatoria—concerning the rights of all foreign merchants trading in England. Apart from its importance it is extremely interesting for the light it throws on the merchandise and trade usages of the period.   From its varied clauses one can gather the difficulties that had beset foreign merchants before the days of charters and privileges, and this charter marked the beginning of the period during

[1] *The Principal Voyages of the English Nation,* Hakluyt, Vol. I, p. 112. (Everyman Edition.)

which foreigners began to enjoy assured safety for themselves and their merchandise.

The following is the text of the Carta Mercatoria as it is given by Hakluyt :

" A mandate of Edward I concerning outlandish merchants.

" We will and command that outlandish marchants doe sel their wares in the citie of London etc., within forty dayes of their arrivale.

" The Great Charter granted unto forreigne marchants by King Edward I in the 31 yeare of his reigne commonly called Carta Mercatoria, anno dominie 1303.

" Edward by the grace of God King of England, Lord of Ireland, Duke of Aquitaine, to Archbishops, Bishops, Abbots, Priors, Earles, Barons, Justices, Vicounts, Governours, Officers and all Bayliffes and his faithful people sendeth greetings. Wee have speciall care for the good estate of all Marchants of the kingdomes, lands and contreis following : to wit of Almaine, France, Spaine, Portugal, Navarre, Lombardie, Florence, Provence, Catalonia, of our Duchie of Aquitaine, Tholosa, Caturlune, Flanders, Brabant, and of all other forreine countreis and places by what name soever they be called, which come into our kingdome of England and there remayne, that the sayd marchants may live in quiet and full securitie under our dominion in time to come. Wherefore that their hearts' desires may bee more readily inclined to our service, and the service of our kingdome, we favourably agreeing to their petitions, for the fuller asring of their estate, have thought good to grant the sayd marchants for us and our heires forever these priviledges under written, ordaining in forme as follows :—

" First that all marchants of the sayd kingdomes and

countreys may come into our kingdome of England,
and anywhere else into our dominion with their
marchandises, whatsoever safely and securely under
our defence and protection without paying wharfage,
pontage or pannage. And that in Cities, Boroughs
and market townes of the sayd kingdome and dominion
they may traffique onely by the great as well with the
naturall subjects and inhabitantes of our aforesayde
kingdome and dominion, as with forreiners, straungers
or private persons. Yet so, that marchandises which
are commonly called mercerie wares, and spices may
be sold by the small, as heretofor hath been accustomed. And that all the aforesaid marchants may
cary or cause to be caried whither they will; (as well)
within our realme or dominion or out of the same ;
saving unto the countries of the manifest and knowne
enemies of our kingdome, those marchandises which
they shall bring into our foresayd realme and dominion,
or buy, or otherwise purchase in our sayd realme and
dominion, paying such customes as they ought to
doe : except onely wines which it shall not be any
wayes lawfull for them to carry out of our sayd realme
and dominion without our speciall favour and licence,
after they be once brought into our realme and
dominion.

" Item that the aforesayd marchants may at their
pleasure lodge and remaine with their goods in the
cities boroughs and townes aforesaid, with the good
liking of those which are owners of their lodgings.

" Item that every bargaine made by the said marchants with any manner of persons, of what places
soever they be, for any kind of marchandise whatsoever, shalbe firme and stable, so that none of both
the marchants shall shrinke or give backe from that
bargaine, after that the earnest penie be once given
and taken betweene the principall bargayners. And if
peradventure any strife arise about the same bargaine,

the trial and inquirie thereof shall be made according to the uses and customes of the fayres and townes where it chanced that the said bargaine was made and contracted.

" Item, we promise the aforesaid marchants granting for ever for us and our heirs, that from hence foorth we will not in any wise make nor cause to be made any stay or arrest, or any delay by reason of arrest of their wares, marchandises or other goods, by our selves, or by any other or others for any neede or accident against the will of the sayd marchants, without present payment of such a price as the marchants would have sold those marchandises for to other men, or without making of them other satisfaction, so that they shall hold themselves well contented : and that no price or valuation shalbe set upon their wares, marchandises and goods by us or by any officer of ours.

" Item, we will that all bayliffes and officers of fayres, cities, boroughs, and market townes shall doe speedie justice from day to day without delay according to the lawe of Marchants to the aforesayd marchants when they shall complaine before them, touching all and singuler causes, which may be determined by the same law. And if default be found in any of the bayliffes or officers aforesayd, whereby the sayd marchants or any of them have sustained, or do sustaine any damage through delay, though the marchant recover his losses against the partie principall, yet the bayliffe or other officer shall be punished to us ward, according to the quality of the default. And wee doe grant this punishment in favour of the aforesayd marchants in regard of the hastening of their justice.

" Item, that in al manner of pleas, saving that in case where punishment of death is to be inflicted, where a marchant is impleaded, or sueth another, of what condition soever hee bee which is sued, whether stranger or home borne, in fayres, cities or boroughs, where sufficient numbers of marchants of the foresayd countreis are, and where the triall ought to bee made, let the one halfe of the Jurie be of the sayd marchants, and the other half of good and lawfull men of the place where the suite shall fall out to bee : and if sufficient number of marchants of the sayd countries cannot bee found, those which shall be found fit in that place shall be put upon the jurie, and the rest shall be chosen of good and fit men of the places where such suit shall chance to be.

" Item, we will, we ordaine, and wee appoint, that in every market towne and fayre of our realme aforesayd and elsewhere within our dominion our weight shall bee set in some certaine place ; and that before the weighing the balance shall be seen emptie in the presence of the buyer and the seller, and that the skales bee equall : and that afterward the weigher weigh in the equal balance. And when he hath set the balances even, let him straightway remoove his hands, so that the balance weigh remayne even : And that throughout all our kingdome and dominion there be one weight and one measure, and that they be marked with the marke of our standard. And that every man may have a weight of one quarter of an hundred, and under, where the same hath not been contrary to the liberty of the lord of the place, and contrary to the libertie granted by us and our predecessors, or contrary to the custome of townes and fayers which hath hitherto been observed.

" Item we will and we grant that some certaine faythfull and discreete man resident in London be appointed to doe Justice to the aforesayd marchants, before whome they may have their sutes decided, and may speedilie recover their debts, if the Sheriffes and Maior should not from day to day give them speedy justice. And hereof let a Commission be made :

which we grant unto the aforesaid marchants besides this present Charter : to wit of such things as betweene marchant and marchant are to be decided according to the lawe of marchants.

"Item we ordayne and appoynt, and wee will that this ordinance and statute shall firmly bee observed for ever for us and our heirs, that the aforesayd marchants shal not lose the aforesayd liberties nor any of them, for any libertie whatsoever, which wee or our heirs hereafter shall grant. And for the obtayning of the aforesayd liberties and free customes, and for the remission of our arresting of their goods, the aforesayd marchants all and every of them for themselves and all other of their parties with one accorde and one consent have granted unto us, that of every tunne of wine, which they shall bring or cause to be brought into our realme and dominion, for which they shall bee bound to pay freight unto the mariners, besides the olde customes which are due and were wont to bee paid unto us, they will pay unto us and to our heirs in the name of a custome two shillings in money, either out of hande, or else within forty days after the sayd wines shall be brought on land out of the shippes. Item for every sacke of wooll, which the sayd marchants or others in their name shall buy and carie out of the realme, or cause to bee brought and carried out, they will pay forty pence above the old custome of halfe a marke, which was payd heretofore : And for a last of hides to bee caryed out of our realme and dominion halfe a marke above that which hereto fore was payd by the olde custome. And likewise for three hundreth Felles with the wooll on them to bee transported out of our realme and dominion fortie pence, above that certaine rate which before was paid by the olde custome : Also two shillings upon every scarlate and every cloth died in graine. Item eighteene pence for every cloth wherein any kind of graine is mingled.

Item twelve pence upon every cloth dyed without graine.
Item twelve pence upon everie quintall of copper.

" And whereas sundrie of the aforesayd marchants
are woont to exercise other marchandises, as of Haver
de pois, and other fine wares, as sarcenets, lawnes,
cindalles, and silke, and divers other marchandises,
and to sell horses and other beastes, corne, and sundrie
other things and marchandises, which cannot easily
bee reduced unto a certaine custome : the sayd marchants have granted to give unto us, and to our heires
of every pound of silver of the estimation and value of
these kinde of goods and marchandises, by what name
soever they be called, three pence in the pound in the
bringing in of these goods into our realme and dominion
aforesaid, within twentie days after these goods and
marchandises shall be brought into our realme and
dominion, and shall be there unladen and solde. And
likewise three pence upon every pound of silver in
the carrying out of any such goods and marchandises
which are bought in our realme and dominion aforesayd
above the customes beforetime payd unto us or any
of our progenitors. And touching the value and
estimation of these goods and marchandises, whereof
three pence of every pound of silver, as is aforesayd,
is to be payd, credite shall be given unto them upon
the letters which they are able to showe from their
masters or parteners. And if they have no letters in
this behalf, we will stand to the othe of the foresayd
marchants if they bee present, or in their absence to
the othes of their servants.

" Moreover, it shall be lawfull for such as be of
the company of the aforesayd marchants within our
realme and dominion aforesayd, to sell woolles to
other of their company and likewise to buy of them
without paying of custome. Yet so, that the said
wools come not to such hands, that wee be defrauded
of the custome due unto us. And furthermore it is

to be understood, that after that the aforesaid marchants have once paid in one place within our realme and dominion, the custome above granted unto us in forme aforesayd for their marchandises, and have their warrant thereof, whether these marchandises remayne within our kingdome or be carried out (excepting wines, which in no wise shalbe carried forth of our realme and dominion aforesaid, without our favour and licence as is aforesayd) we wil and we grant for us and our heires, that no execution, attachment, or loane, or any other burthen be layd upon the persons of the aforesayd marchants, upon their marchandises or goods in any case, contrary to the forme before mentioned and granted. The faithfull and principall witnesses of these presents are these, Robert Archbishop Canterbury, Primate of all England, Walter bishop of Coventrey and Lichfield, Henry Lacie of Lincolne, Humfrey de Bohume, Earle of Herford and Essex, high Constable of England, Adomare of Valentia, Geofrey of Gaymal, Hugh Spenser, Walter Beauchampe, Seneschall of our house, Robert of Bures and others. Given by our own hand at Windesore the first day of February in the yere of our reigne xxxi."[1]

The quarrels and reconciliations between the Hansa and England continued throughout the reigns of Henry VI and Edward IV, and with the development of the English trading spirit the kings were obliged more and more to curtail the privileges of the League.

During the long struggle of the Hansa with France, many of their ships were seized by the English, and the League retaliated by sending ships to harry the east coast, where many English were taken prisoner

[1] *The Principal Voyages of the English Nation*, Hakluyt, Vol. I, pp. 113-17. (Everyman Edition.)

and treated with extreme brutality by the Germans. Cologne was un-Hansed for her dislike of this policy. But peace was eventually made and Edward IV gave the League good terms in England.

It was largely through the clever diplomacy of Heinrich Murmeister, a member of the Hansa Diet, that this peace was eventually brought about and ratified by the signing of the famous Treaty of Utrecht in 1447, which gave the English merchants the same rights in Hanseatic cities abroad that the Germans enjoyed in England ; rights which, however, were never acknowledged by the League—a fact which led to serious trouble with Elizabeth. The terms of this treaty were used later on by the town of Hamburg as a basis for their defence of their right to harbour English merchants.

But there were still quarrels, and by now the English kings were beginning to feel themselves powerful enough to insist on their subjects being better treated abroad. Henry VII was the first to take a decisive step when, in 1492, he forbade the export of wool by Germans.

HANSEATIC PEWTERS

CHAPTER XIII

DISPUTES BETWEEN THE ORDER OF TEUTONIC KNIGHTS
AND THE ENGLISH KINGS

ALTHOUGH it is beyond dispute that the majority of the carrying trade of the period was in the hands of foreign merchants—mainly the merchants of Almaine—it must never for a moment be imagined that there were no English ships trading to Europe.

In the days of the leagues of cities there is much evidence of the English faring to Bergen, Scånia, Novgorod and Bruges, and it was only with the gradual rise of the united Hanseatic League, with its constant desire for monopoly, that our merchants began to experience more and more difficulty in carrying on a peaceful trade in foreign cities.

The reign of Edward II saw the beginnings of the Hanseatic League as a united power, and with it came troublous times for the English merchants.

Despite the many safe-conducts issued to foreign merchants in England on the condition that our traders received equal rights abroad, there were constant complaints of evil treatment at the hands of Prussian and German merchants, either in their own countries or in Norway and Scånia.

It was a fixed principle of the Hanseatic League

never to grant reciprocal terms to foreign merchants in its own cities, and this was one of the main causes of its eventual downfall.

The first troubles arose in Norway, and Edward carried on a long correspondence with the king in order to see his subjects fairly treated :

" We are much disquieted in our cogitations considering the greevances and oppressions, which (as wee have beene informed by pityful complaintes) are at present, <u>more than in times past</u>, without any reasonable cause inflicted upon our subjects, which doe usually resort unto your Kingdome for traffiques sake."

It would seem that three English ships, having been loaded with salt herrings and other commodities, in the town of Tonnesberg, the " said mariners, men and servants of the aforesaid shippes, being licensed by virtue of the safe-conduct that you have granted them, freely to return unto the parts of England with their ships and goods aforesaid," were seized by the bailiffs of the district.

The ships, having been detained in Norwegian waters by contrary winds, were seized after the murder of a certain bailiff of Vikia by pirates and malefactors upon the sea, and were held till such time as they could find surety for a fine of forty pounds sterling for each ship ; and also till they provided three pledges each that they would return with their ships to the same harbour before the Feast of John the Baptist next.

Edward points out that it is against all right and justice that such persons and their goods shall be seized for the delinquencies of other individuals with whom they had nothing whatever to do ; and begs for their instant release.

Evidently nothing was done in the matter, for two more letters were written, urging the release of the prisoners held in

" the town of Northbern (Bergen) . . . by which close prison, lack of due nourishment and extremetie of loathsomeness many, we understand have quite perished. . . . How be it, you retaining as yet our marchants endurance as before, in your letters, which we have diligently read, and thoroughly understood, have amongst other matters, returned this answer to us : that certaine marchants of your kingdome doe make sunderie complaints of injuries whereby they have lately (as themselves avouch) contrary to justice, beene agrieved and oppressed in our dominions adding moreover in your said letter, that certaine sonnes of iniquitie of the towne of Lenne, comming, as they saide, to fish for herrings cruelly murthered a certaine Knight, who was in times past your bailiffe of Vikia, together with ten others of your subjects, . . . giving you for a certaintie to understand, that if upon lawful inquisition we shal be advertised of any such grievences which have bene offered unto your subjects within our realme, we will cause speedie justice to be administered, and sufficient recompence and due satisfaction to be made in regard thereof . . . and that the deliverie of our foresaide marchants and goods may be the more easily yielded unto, may it please you with dilligent observation to consider that Gefferey Drew and certaine other of our marchants of Lenne upon occasion of the greivances offered unto your marchants within our realme (as the report goeth) at the suite of Tidman Lippe, paide unto the same your marchants an hundreth pound sterling ; even as in a

certain Indenture made between Ingelram Lende of
Thorenden, and some other of your marchants of the
one part, and between the aforesayde Geffrey, and
certaine of our marchants on the other, wee sawe
conteined. Moreover, if any of your subjects be
minded to exhibite, and effectually to prosecute their
complaints in our Courts, concerning any of our
subjects, or of any injury done unto them, we will
cause the petitions of those your subjects to be admitted, and also full and speedie justice to be administered upon any such like complaints of theirs."[1]

Exactly the same troubles continued for years, each
country sending letters of complaint, and then patching
up more or less satisfactory agreements ; but, under-
lying the whole matter, was the League jealousy of
the foreign traders and its unwillingness to give equal
privileges and protection to the English merchants in
their midst. With the steady rise of the Hanseatic
League matters grew more and more serious, for
England was not strong enough to insist on the Germans withdrawing if they did not amend their treatment of her merchants abroad.

Edward III, who was notorious for his fondness
for foreigners, had a marked predilection for the
Hansa. He was perpetually in need of money and
more than once the German merchants came to his
aid. When he found himself in difficulties after the
failure of the famous Italian banking house of Bardi,
he borrowed largely from the League, one record
stating that they lent him no less than 35,000
livres.

[1] *The Principal Voyages of the English Nation*, Hakluyt, Vol. I,
pp. 121-2. (Everyman Edition.)

He constantly proclaimed his liking for the Hansa and made great favourites of two League representatives, one a burgomaster of Lübeck, who came as ambassador for the Hansa to arrange for the continuance of League privileges ; the other, Simon Swerting, a citizen of Lübeck, and an influential member of the Hansa, who was for many years their representative in London.

But after the reign of Edward III far more serious trouble was to arise. At that time the Order of Teutonic Knights had assumed great temporal power, and had entered into an agreement with the Hanseatic League throughout the North German and Prussian cities. After many complaints by the Prussian merchants of ill-treatment at the hands of the English, the Grand Master of the Order, Conradus Zolner de Rotinstein, sent an embassage to England to demand satisfaction. He maintained that their goods had been seized and their persons injured ; whereupon certain goods of the English merchants in Prussia were confiscated. He further begged the King to send his ambassadors to Prussia to deal with the matter.

So in August, 1388, the King's ambassadors, Master Nicholas Stocket, Licentiate in both lawes, Thomas Graa and Walter Sibill, citizens of London and Yorke, together with John Bevis of London, their informer, with sufficient authority and full commandment to handle, discuss and finally determine the foresaid business where received by the Master General at his castle at Marienburg.

Everything went off very well, they were treated

with courtesy and friendliness and came to a satisfactory agreement. The injured Prussian merchants
were to return to England with the ambassadors to
lay their complaints before the King, when he promised
to see that they received full justice and amendment ;
at the same time the English merchants were to put
their complaints before the Master General.

The English cases were to be heard in the city of
Danzig before two deputies from Elbing and two of
Danzig. The freedom of English merchants through-
out Prussia and of Prussian merchants throughout
England, with all their old privileges of trade, were
guaranteed by the Grand Master and Richard II.

Matters having been successfully adjusted for the
time being, trade continued, but it was not long before
fresh quarrels arose, and this time the negotiations
between Prussia and England were long and complicated.

In 1403, Conradus de Juningen, the famous Master
of the Teutonic Knights, sent ambassadors to Henry
IV, to ask for amends and recompense for injuries
offered to merchants of his country, the sum-total
demanded being 19,120 nobles.

Finding that his letters were not well received by
the Grand Master, Henry decided to send an embassage
to Prussia and the Hansa towns. After this decision,
and pending the arrival of the ambassadors in Prussia,
trade intercourse between the two countries was
suspended. English merchants in Prussia were forbidden to remove their goods from port under pain
of forfeit, and were ordered to sell them in the ports
to Prussians only, (that is to Hanseats, who were under

the joint protection of the League and the Knights Teutonic).

After the arrival of the ambassadors, the English merchants might once again freely visit all parts with their merchandise and sell it according to their ancient privileges.

When negotiations opened, the English ambassadors brought forward a claim for 4,535 nobles, which sum they maintained was due for injuries received by English merchants at the hands of Prussians; upon which the Grand Master claimed an extra sum of 5,100 nobles in addition to the 19,120 nobles claimed by his ambassadors in England.

And so it went on, each side claiming vast sums for damages done to its merchants. The whole proceedings were incredibly intricate, as clauses had to be included to cover any claims that had already been settled, and other claims the authenticity of which was denied. The King of England demanded that the damage should be assessed by an uninterested party:

" provided alwayes, that the value and price of all wares, goods and marchandises, whereof the said citizens and marchants of Livonia, in their articles received by the sayde English ambassadours, as is aforesayd, doe make mention, shall be justly esteemed, prized and approved, not by any of England or of Prussia or of Livonia, but by some other indifferent marchants of good credite, valuing them at the true rate of marchants, which sayd like marchandise would have amounted unto if at the time when they were taken, they had bene to be solde at the town of Bruges in Flanders."

Henry also asked for better treatment of the English merchants while in Hansa territory, with a very particular emphasis on the Baltic fishing grounds :

" Our desire is in particular, that our marchants and liege subjects may have more free passage granted them unto the parts of Scånia, for the providing of herrings and of other fishes there, that they may there remaine, and from thence also may more securely returne unto their own home : and we beseech you in consideration of our owne selves that you would have our marchants and leige subjects especially recommended unto you, safely protecting them (if need shall require) under the shadow of your defence ; even as you would have us deale in the like case with your own subjects."

In the end it was finally decided that by May, 1406, satisfaction should be given by both countries, and that if this was not carried out all Prussian merchants should leave England within three months, free passage for themselves, their ships and their goods being guaranteed—the same should apply to all English merchants within the realm of the Grand Master.

The ambassadors were to meet at the town of Dordrecht in Holland for the settlement of this business.

On their return journey to England the ambassadors were to visit the chief towns of the Hansa merchants to confer with the various burgomasters concerning the payments of all claims for damages.

During the years of this embassage there was an important meeting between the English ambassadors and the ambassadors of the Grand Master of the Teutonic Knights and the Hansa Cities. This took place at the Hague on August 28th, 1407, and once again the claims of the Grand Master were examined and were admitted by all members of the convention to be of a " certaine obscurity."

It was again decided that, pending a satisfactory settlement, trade between Prussia and England should cease.

At the same time an agreement was made between Henry IV and the " Common Society of the Marchants of the Hans." It was concluded between the English ambassadors and representatives of the cities of Lübeck, Bremen, Hamburg, Sund and Grifeswald, and guaranteed satisfaction for their claims for damages and also the claims of other cities, towns and villages of the Hans . . .

" and that the liege marchants and subjects of our sayd soverign lord the king, and the marchants of the Common Society of the Dutch Hans aforesaid, from hence forth for one whole yeere and seven months immediately next ensueing and following shall be permitted and licensed freely friendly and securely to exercise mutual traffic, and like marchants to buy and sell together one of and unto another, even as in times past, namely in the year 1400 and before that time also, they have been accustomed to exercise mutual traffic and marchandise and to buy and sell."

These diplomatic meetings took place between 1403 and 1409, and it was at the Dordrecht meeting in 1405 that England produced her various claims for the damage done by the Victual Brother pirates, and during the sack of Bergen in 1394, when twenty-one houses belonging to the English merchants were burnt. As an offset to these the Grand Master claimed damages for outrages offered to his merchants.

" Item by the inhabitants of Scardeburgh, Blakeney and Crowmer (who had one John Jolly of Blakeney for their captaine) 156 nobles which are due unto Henry Culeman . . . item by the inhabitants of Plymouth and Dertmouth (whose captaines were Henry Pay and William Gadeling) 600 nobles which are due to John Halewater in respect of his goods by them violently taken away . . . item that Sir William de Etheringham, Knight, who was vice admirall for the sea, must bee summoned to alleage a reasonable cause (for that the sayd Sir William and his servants expelled the said John Halewater out of his ship for the space of fifteene dayes together, and took of the goods and victual of the said John to the summe of 114 nobles) why he ought not to pay the said summe of 114 nobles unto John Halewater aforesaid : which if hee shall not bee willing nor able to alleage before the first of April next ensueing, that then by the king's authoritie hee must be compelled to pay unto the aforesaid John the said 114 nobles. Item by John Bilis neer unto Crowmer 68 nobles which are due unto Nicholas Wolmersten of Elbing . . . item it is covenanted and granted that the heirs of Lord Henrie de Percy, the Yonger, after they shall come unto lawfull age and shall have obtained unto the possessions and goods of their inheritance, must be compelled by the king's authoritie (justice going before) to make satisfaction unto the Great Procurator of Marienburgh with the summe of 838 nobles in lieu of certaine corne and graine which the aforesaid Lord Henrie, in the yeer 1403, bought and received of the said Great Procuratur, for the use of the castle Zutberwik." [1]

[1] Various excerpts from Hakluyt, *English Voyages*, Vol. I, pp. 168-70.

These are only five out of the large number of claims, but together with our demands against the injuries done to Englishmen by the " pirates and malefactors of the Hans " they serve to show the keen rivalry that existed between the English and the German merchants, and that, although so rich and powerful, the Hanseatic League found the English traders a considerable menace to their system of monopoly.

A very important point arising from these merchant troubles was Henry IV's realization of the difficulties of English merchants abroad. In 1403 he granted a charter to all English merchants resident in Prussia, Denmark, Norway, Sweden and Germany, by which he allowed them to choose their own governors from amongst their ranks ; the governors to have rights of ruling all English merchants, resident or visiting, and of settling disputes among themselves as well as disputes between the English merchants and the natives of the land ; together with the right of demanding satisfaction from the rulers of the countries, according to the ancient privileges prevailing in the land of residence.

This power of government and arbitration by merchants living on the spot must have greatly facilitated matters in all cases of confiscation of goods and claims for indemnification.

Thus by the end of Henry IV's reign the Hanseatic League was at the height of its power and, in its selfish desire for monopoly, was making itself felt in every trading centre from Bergen to London. Its Kontors in Bergen, Bruges and Novgorod were rich and flourishing, and they held an almost undisputed monopoly of the northern carrying trade, and the fishing industry in the Baltic. The power of the League in England was great (all the foregoing correspondence shows that the English were not yet strong enough to insist on the rights of their merchants abroad, by taking decisive action against the German merchants in England) ; and its Kontor at the Steelyard was to persist long after the other European Kontors had fallen from their high estate.

SAND-SHAKER

CHAPTER XIV

THE EARLY HISTORY OF THE STEELYARD

ALTHOUGH the German merchants had a depot in London from the tenth century onward, it was not until the reign of Richard II that it was known as the Steelyard.

In 1155 it is referred to as the " Haus zu Colner," in London ; in 1194 as the " Gildehalle die Colner " ; in 1224 as the " Guildehalle Theutonicorum," or Guildhall of the Teutonics ; and in 1409 as the " Hall of the Easterlings," or the " Easterlings Halle."

Thus, by the name alone, one can trace the gradual growth and spread of their trade, as the Hanseatic League developed. At first it was mainly the men of Cologne who visited London, then merchants from various parts of Germany, and finally, with the development of the Baltic trade, were added the " Easterlings " (men from the " Östsjö " or Baltic), who came into close touch with London through the rich League city of Visby, in Gotland.

Much controversy has ranged round the possible origin of the name Steelyard. Some authorities insist that it was so called because it was the London repository for the iron and steel brought to England by the Hanseatic merchants.

This is quite possible, as it might be a corruption

164

of the Danish " Staal," German " Stahl," Old English " Style," all meaning steel ; and may very probably have been called by the Easterlings, the " Staalgaard," or " Staalgård," thus coming directly into English as " Styleyard " ; just as the word " gardens " came to be applied to the Bergen Kontor.

This theory seems to be supported by the fact that Mineshew, in his Dictionary, gives the meaning of " Steelyard " as " A broad place or court wherein steel was much sold." Stow, in his *Survey of London*, refers to the depot of the " Haunce of Almaine " as the " Steel house."

Other authorities claim that the place was so named from its being the spot in which was kept the great " Stilyard," or weighing beam, of the City of London. That one great beam was kept in the Steelyard in Thames Street is beyond dispute, but it is also indisputable that there was more than one. A charter of Henry VIII, given on April 13th, 1531, cites Sir William Sidney as

" keeper of the great beam, balance and weight at the Stillyard ; also to the Mayor, Communalty and citizens of our citie, authority and power to make, name and assign, from time to time, all manner of clerks, porters, servants and ministers of the great beam and balance, and of the iron beam and of the beam of the Stillyard, and of all weights thereof."

But many German authorities, among them Lappenburg,[1] deny both these origins, and assert that the word Steelyard had nothing to do with either steel or

[1] Lappenburg, *Urkundliche Geschichte des Hansischen Stahlhofes zu London* . . . Hamburg, 1851.

the weighing beam, but that it was derived from " Stollgeld "—in English " Stallagium "—the name given to a tax paid on the merchandise exposed for sale in a " Stahlhof," the Stahlhof being the open space in front of a guildhall or merchant's house. At Damme, in Flanders, the square outside the covered merchants' shops was called the " Stahlhof."

Whatever the origin of the name, the fact remains that in all the City of London archives, the house of the merchants of Almaine is written as Stelyard, Stillyard, Stilyerd, Styleyard, Stillyerd, Stylleyarde, and never as Stahlhof, and that the same word, in its variations, is used for the great beam or weighing arm.

The Steelyard was situated in the Dowgate ward of London ; and the original house of the Germans was probably of no great size, but as the power of the Hanseatic League increased, and their privileges and charters were confirmed by successive English Kings, they bought up many of the adjoining properties, till the Kontor occupied a large area.

In return for their valuable privileges the German merchants of the Steelyard undertook to repair and rebuild the Bishopsgate, and to defend it, if such were required.

In Stow's *Survey of London* three occasions are mentioned when this was done. The first, in 1282, which occurs in his general description of the Steelyard ; the second in 1479, in the reign of Edward IV, when " the gate was again beautifully built by the Haunce merchants " ; and the third

" about the year 1551, when these Haunce merchants, having prepared stone for that purpose, caused a new gate to be framed, there to have been set up, but then their liberties, through suite of our English merchants, were seized unto the King's hands ; and so the work was stayed and the old gate yet remaineth."

The following is Stow's description of the Steelyard :

" Next to this lane,[1] on the east, is the Steelyard, as they term it, a place for merchants of Almaine, that used to bring hither as well wheat, rye, and other grain, as cables, ropes, masts, pitch, tar, flax, hemp, linen, cloth, wainscots, wax, steel, and other profitable merchandises. Unto these merchants, in the year 1259, Henry III, at the request of his brother Richard, Earl of Cornewell, king of Almaine, granted that all and singular the merchants, having a house in the city of London, commonly called ' Guilda Aula Theutonicorum,' should be maintained and upholden, through the whole realm, by all such freedoms, and free usages, or liberties, as by the king and his noble progenitors' time they had and enjoyed, etc. Edward I renewed and confirmed that charter of liberties granted by his father. And in the 10th year of the same Edward, Henry Wales being mayor,[2] a great controversy did arise between the said mayor, and the merchants of the Haunce of Almaine, about the reparations of Bishopsgate, then likely to fall, for that the said merchants enjoyed divers privileges in respect of maintaining the said gate, which they now denied to repair ; for the appeasing of which controversy the king sent his writ to the treasurer and barons of his Exchequer, commanding that they should make inquisition thereof ; before whom the merchants being called, when they were not able to discharge them-

---

[1] Cosin Lane. (Author's note.)
[2] 1282. (Author's note.)

selves, sith they enjoyed the liberties to them granted
for the same, a precept was sent to the mayor and
sheriffs to distrain the said merchants to make reparations, namely, Gerard Marbod, alderman of the
Haunce, Ralph de Cussarde, a citizen of Colen,
Ludero de Denevar, a burgess of Trivar, John of Aras,
a burgess of Trivon, Bartram of Hamburdge, Gode-
stalke of Hundondale, a burgess of Trivon, John de
Dele, a burgess of Munstar, then remaining in the
said city of London, for themselves and all other
merchants of the Haunce, and so they granted 210
marks sterling to the mayor and citizens, and undertook that they and their successors should from time
to time repair the said gate, and bear the third part
of the charges in money and men to defend it when
need were. And for this agreement the said mayor
and citizens granted to the said merchants their
liberties, which till of late they have enjoyed, as
namely, amongst other, that they might lay up their
grain, which they brought into this realm in inns, and
sell it in their garners, by the space of forty days after
they had laid it up, except by the mayor and citizens
they were expressly forbidden, because of dearth, or
other reasonable occasions. Also they might have
their aldermen as they had been accustomed, fore-
seeing always that he were of the city, and presented
to the mayor and aldermen of the city, so oft as any
should be chosen, and should take an oath before
them to maintain justice in their courts, and to behave
themselves in their office according to law, and as it
stood with the customs of the city.

" Thus much for their privileges ; whereby it
appeareth that they were great merchants of corn
brought out of the east parts hither, insomuch that
the occupiers of husbandry in this land were enforced
to complain of them for bringing in such abundance,
when the corn of this realm was at such an easy price ;

whereupon it was ordained by parliament, that no person should bring into any part of this realm, by way of merchandise, wheat, rye, or barley, growing out of the said realm, when the quarter of wheat exceed not the price of 6s. 8d., rye 4s. the quarter, and barley 3s. the quarter, upon forefeiture the one half to the king, and the other half to the seizor thereof. These merchants of Haunce had their Guildhall in Thames street in place aforesaid by the said Cosin lane. Their hall is large, built of stone, with three arched gates towards the street, the middlemost whereof is far bigger than the other, and is seldom opened, the other two be mured up ; the same is now called the old hall.

" Of later time, to wit, in the 6th of Richard II,[1] they hired one house next adjoining to their old hall which sometime belonged to Richard Lions, a famous lapidary, one of the sheriffs of London, in the 49th of Edward III,[2] and in the 4th of Richard II [3] by the rebels of Kent, drawn out of that house and beheaded in West Cheap. This also was a great house with a large wharf on the Thames, and the way thereunto was called Windgoose, or Wildgoose lane, which is now called Windgoose alley, for that the same alley is for the most part built on by the Stilyard merchants.

" The abbot of St. Alban's had a messuage here with a key given to him in the 34th of Henry VI.[4] Then is one other great house, which sometime pertained to John Rainwell, Stockfishmonger, mayor, and it was by him given to the Mayor and commonalty, to the end that the profits thereof should be disposed in deeds of piety ; which house in the 15th of Edward IV [5] was confirmed unto the said merchants, in manner following, namely :—' It is ordayned by our soverigne

---

[1] 1382. (Author's note.)   [2] 1375. (Author's note.)
[3] 1380. (Author's note.)   [4] 1455. (Author's note.)
          [5] 1475. (Author's note.)

lord and his parliament, that the said marchants of Almaine, being of the companie called the Guildhall Teutonicorum (or the Flemish gild), that now be, or hereafter shall be, shall have, hold and enjoy, to them and their successors for ever, the said place called the Steel house, yeelding to the said mayor and communaltie an annuall rent of £70 3s. 4d. etc.'

"In the year 1551, and the 5th of Edward VI, through complaint of the English merchants, the liberty of the steelyard merchants was seized into the king's hands, and so it resteth." [1]

Touching the Hansa obligation to defend Bishopsgate in case of need there is an interesting record in the Journals of the Courts of Aldermen :

"A hundred pounds paid to Hanse Brand, of the Stilyard, to declare such of their members as have cross-bows and hand guns."

In the civic records of the Guildhall archives there is the following record of the lease of the Steelyard :

"A lease of the Stilyard to be made to the Treasurer of England, Sir John Lay and Richard Fowler, from Michaelmas to Easter, £70.3.4., and of the tenement belonging to the Priory of Elsings Spitel, for 32 years at £13.16.8., with power to distrain for rent in arrears."

In 1332, William Elsing, a mercer of the City of London, founded Elsings Spitel, in Cripplegate. The above-mentioned tenement was, in all probability, a house that had been left to the Foundation by some later bequest, and was, almost certainly, one of the

[1] *The Survey of London*, by John Stow, pp. 208–10. 1581. (Everyman Edition.)

houses in Thames Street adjoining the Steelyard, as there are no records of the Hanseatic League possessing scattered property in the City.

A notable feature of the Hanseatic Kontor was the Cosin's Garden Tavern—not that it was a tavern in the correct sense of the word, but rather a modification of a German Beer-garden.

Between the old Guildhall, with its tower, where the archives of the organization were kept, and the Kontor-master's house on the river-front, ran a long garden, grassed and planted with fruit trees, and carefully tended by the members. Here, at tables placed under the shady trees, the members of the Steelyard sold their foreign delicacies, caviare, smoked salmon, sturgeon, and good Rhenish wine at sixpence a gallon.

The company at Cosin's Garden must have been many and varied. There the stately Hanseatic merchants sat with their friends and arranged many a profitable transaction, while the younger members of the Kontor waited on the company.

But apart from business, Cosin's Garden was a resort of many of the notabilities of the day. Probably Shakespeare, Marlowe and Henslow met their noble patrons at the Rhenish wine-house, to discuss their plays over many a tankard.

In the literature of the period there are many references to this tavern. For instance, in *Pierce Pennilesse*, a character says :

" Men when they idle and know not what to do sayeth one to another, lets to the Stillyard and drink Rhenish wine " ;

while John Webster's "Industriano" appoints a meeting of scholars with Sir Gosling Glow-worm:

"I entreat you to meet him this afternoon at the Rhenish warehouse in the Stillyard. Will you steal forth and taste a Dutch brew and a keg of sturgeon?"

In *Pepys's Diary* there are three references to the Rhenish wine-house:

Aug. 1660. "With Judge Advocate, Fowler, Mr. Creed and Mr. Shepley, to the Rhenish wine house."
Nov. 24, 1660. "Creed, Sheply and I to the Rhenish wine house, and there I did buy them two quarts of worm-wood wine." [1]
May, 1661. "To the Rhenish wine house and there Mr. Jonas Moore, the mathmatician, to us." [2]

There is only one reference in *Pepys's* to the Steelyard; in October, 1665:

"To the Still Yard, which place is now however shut up of the Plague, but I was there, and we now make no bones of it."

Cosin's Garden, together with a great proportion of the Thames Street buildings, was destroyed in the Great Fire of 1666, when the Kontor master only just escaped with his life.

The civic archives at the Guildhall contain many

---

[1] Crème d'absinthe.
[2] There appear to have been two Rhenish wine-houses, the other in Crooked Lane, Thames Street. I have found no evidence that both these Rhenish taverns belonged to the Hanseats, although the latter was owned by foreigners. Neither is it probable, as the Steelyard seems to have had no separate buildings scattered throughout the City.

records of the jealously guarded privilege of selling by retail. The Hanseats, in the reign of Edward III, were evidently given this privilege, vide the following record :

"Writ to the Sherifs to make proclamation of Letters Patent, granted by the King at the Cities' request, to the effect that, thence forth no stranger shall sell by retail in the City and suburbs, or be tenant of a Hostal, or be a broker, saveing always to the merchants of the Hanse of Almaine their liberties.

"Witness the King at Westminster, 4th December."

With the growing dislike of the citizens of London for the privileged foreigners, pressure was brought to bear on the civic authorities to compel them to use their influence with the King to get these privileges rescinded. That this was frequently done is evident by the following two records :

"The merchants of the Hanse, Bartholemew de Lon, Bertram de Wypperford, Tydemann, Lymbergh, John de Wolde, Henry de Braken, Richard Sotherlond, Engelbert de Colon, Gerard de Ecof, John Conken, Rudeker, Lymbergh, Sigrid Mayenberg and others, presented a petition to be allowed to continue selling wines retail. Permission was refused." [1]

Then again in 1495 :

"A person of the Stillyarde with the Nudegate serjeant-at-law, came to show sufficient authority to sell wines retail." [2]

Letters were produced and all formalities gone through ; and in the end a command was given to the

[1] Callender of Plea and Memoranda Rolls.
[2] Repertories of the Courts of Aldermen.

" clerks of the Stillyarde " to declare to the Company there that they were to sell no more Rhenish wine within their place by retail.

That at a later date these privileges were reinstated is evident from the popularity of the Rhenish tavern in the Steelyard up to the time of the Fire of London.

The whole history of the Steelyard is a tale of constantly recurring petty quarrels between the Hanseats and the citizens of London, and more than once the Steelyard was attacked. In 1492 when Henry VII had forbidden the export of wool by Hanseatic merchants, an enraged mob attacked the Steelyard, but the plucky, if unscrupulous German merchants defended themselves nobly, and held the building until they were relieved by the Lord Mayor. Stow in his *Survey of London* asserts that this riot upon the Easterlings was led by the Mercers' servants.

In the Guildhall archives there is a letter of 1378 in which the merchants of Almaine complain bitterly of being deprived of their ancient rights and privileges and of being molested by the citizens of London. They desire the Civic authorities to use their good offices with the King to secure them better treatment, otherwise it will behove the said merchants to cease to visit England. Dated Saturday the Feast of Corpus Christi, June 17th, 1378, Dantzic.

An answer was sent, under the seal of the Mayoralty of the City, stating that the privileges of the merchants of Almaine had been suspended by order of Parliament for injuries done to the King's subjects at Scone.[1]

This was the policy of the Hanseatic League in

[1] Scånia, in Sweden. (Author's note.)

Novgorod, Bergen, Bruges and London. Whenever their privileges were curtailed or suspended they promptly threatened to leave the country—without ever really intending to do so—and at that period England was not strong enough to do without them.

As the times grew less troublous and the League richer and more powerful, the prosperous members, generally much travelled men, whose taste in art and culture had been developed by visits to Venice and Bruges, turned their attention towards decorating their Kontor in London.

They ornamented the great hall of the Steelyard with carvings and frescoes, portraits and paintings.

Holbein, who was pre-eminently the painter of the Hansa, was commissioned to paint two large pictures for the Steelyard. They were two allegorical subjects representing the Triumph of Riches and the Triumph of Poverty. They are said to have been extremely fine, but unfortunately they perished, after passing out of the hands of the League, during the period of its decline in England; but engravings made from them are still to be seen in the British Museum.

The Steelyard Kontor possessed a magnificent collection of silver plate which, when the declining League found itself in money difficulties, was sent to Lübeck, where, according to a record in the archives of that city, it was sold, in 1609, for 1,068 thalers.

The great hall was used for all Kontor functions, including the meetings of the Aldermen and Council, and also as a common dining-room (corresponding to the Schütting in the Bergen Kontor).

The Hanseats in London did not possess a church

of their own as they did in Visby, Bergen and Novgorod; probably because they lived more peaceably in England and were allowed to worship undisturbed. They attended the church of All Hallows the More, the Church of the Seamen, in Thames Street, adjacent to the Steelyard. There they had an altar of their own, where they celebrated special masses, and where great candles of pure wax were kept constantly burning; richly carved pews and stalls were specially reserved for the Aldermen and Council.

In England, the astute Hanseats changed their religion to suit the ruling monarch. When, for instance, in 1526, Sir Thomas More was sent with a body of men to search the Steelyard for the heretical writings of Luther, nothing incriminating was found, but all the Kontor members took the oath as non-heretics; but after the Reformation the members of that same Kontor were attending All Hallows the More as ardent Protestants.

The funeral of a Hanseat, in 1558, is quaintly described in *Machyn's Diary*:

" The XX day of September was bered at Gret All (Hollues) in Temstreet the Altherman of the Steleard with IJ whyte branches and XIJ torchys and IIIJ gret tapurs."

The organization of the Steelyard Kontor was on exactly the same lines as that of the Kontors at Novgorod, Bergen and Bruges. The same laws were enforced and the same fines and punishments inflicted, but in London, as at Bruges, there could be no question of the rough, brutal practices in vogue in Bergen.

In the Steelyard there were the same ranks among the members, the same fixed duration of residence, and the rules of strict celibacy and non-fraternization were sternly insisted upon.

Here the Kontor members were divided into three groups : in the first were the men of Cologne, in the second those of Westphalia, and in the third those of Livonia, Gotland and Prussia.

From the evidence available it is conclusive that the London Kontor was far smaller than that of Bruges, for it had only one Alderman and a Council of twelve.

The Steelyard Alderman had to be a freeman of the City of London and take his oath before the Lord Mayor.

In the Memoranda of the Court Rolls of the Guild-hall Archives, the following record appears :

" In 1282 a corporation granted to the Hanse merchants the enjoyment of their ancient liberties in London, freedom from murage, permission to sell grain for forty days after its arrival, and the right of choosing their own alderman to hold their courts on condition that he be a freeman of the City and take his oath before the Mayor and Aldermen on his election."

The Alderman and Council were elected yearly on New Year's Day ; the council being chosen thus— the members from Cologne chose four men from Westphalia, the Westphalians chose four men from Prussia and the Prussians chose four from the remainder.

No one had a right to refuse office ; the punishment

for the first such offence was a fine and for the second un-Hansing.

They chose their Aldermen by secret vote ; the newly elected Alderman received the keys from his predecessor and took his oath, he then received the oath of the newly elected Council. The Alderman and Council met in the great hall of the Steelyard every Wednesday to conduct the business of the week and to settle all disputes between Hanseats ; these latter were never supposed to take their grievances into the English courts.

The duties of the Alderman and Council were many and arduous. In addition to settling disputes and arranging all business matters of the interior Kontor life, they had to collect tolls and dues from the various cities represented. One of their most important tasks was to see that no non-Hanseat availed himself of League privileges. In the event of a foreign merchant being caught in this heinous crime, the Alderman fined him heavily ; often more heavily than he would have been fined in the English courts for evading Customs or other duties.

Although the Hanseatic League was very quick in preventing rival merchants sheltering under their special liberties, they did occasionally allow non-Hanseats to avail themselves of their protection ; doubtless on due payment of hush-money.

As in the other Kontors, the lower ranks of the Steelyard might be non-Hanseats, if they were of German birth ; but they might do no business for themselves, nor might they mix with the upper ranks, nor fraternize with the English, till after a residence of seven years and their entrance into full Hanseatic status.

In the London and Bruges Kontors there is no evidence of any initiatory tests for apprentices.

The business of the Hanseatic depots at Hull, Boston, Lynn, Grimsby, Southampton, Yarmouth, Canterbury, Rochester, York, Norwich and Bristol, passed to a great extent through the headquarters Kontor of the Steelyard.

Apart from their importance as records of the far-reaching power of the Hanseatic League, the documents in the various civic archives possess a very human interest.

Such strange stilted letters telling their tale of the petty spites and jealousies of rival merchants, separated by the difference of race, and ever striving to get the better of one another. Some documents revealing the cheating that went on under the cloak of the League, others the minute care with which the Hansa looked after its own, to the extent of badgering Lord Mayors, and even Kings, for the restitution of a paltry five pounds' worth of goods ; and yet others ringing with the arrogance of the League of merchants that set itself on an equality with kings and emperors, and dared to dictate terms to them—and, what is still more extraordinary, were powerful enough to get their terms enforced. I can only give a few examples, but there are many more, just as interesting, in all the countries where the Hanseatic League was supreme. From them it will be evident that merchants have changed very little with the centuries, and their methods still less, the great difference being that in these days they do not have to be so bold and so courageous as those old seafaring folk, and that their lives nowadays are hedged in with still more care and protection than even the mighty Hansa could offer.

" A Dutchman, having a ship laden with Bay salt, driven by Tempest, as it was said, into the Thames wished to have the salt away without any price being fixed by the Mayor. The court was not agreeable to this application. The Merchants of the Stillyerd and the Merchants with the Hulk with Bay salt, came to court. It was agreed that the Merchants should be allowed to sell." [1]

Presumably without the price being fixed by the court and without any toll being demanded by the authorities.

The Hansa claimed that if any life escaped from a stranded ship, were it only a cat or dog, the authorities of the land where it was wrecked should have no right to claim either the ship or the cargo.

" To JOHN DE BEAUCHAMP, Admiral of the South,
" Certifying that Servoise Gomans, merchant of Dynaunt [2] who had complained that his goods had been seized by the mayor and bailifs of Dover, in the ship John Petresonne of Lesclus (Sluys) they believing him to be a freeman of the city of London, he is not free of the same, but resides in the said city as a merchant stranger of the Hanse of Almaine." London, 10th June, 1349. [3]

Presumably the authorities at Dover seized his goods because he had not paid toll on them, but as a

---

[1] Repertories of the Court of Aldermen.
[2] Dinant, on the Meuse. (Author's note.)
[3] Letter Books of the City of London.

privileged merchant of the Hansa he would be exempt from paying.

All the old authorities insist on the fact that the Hanseatic merchant must be of German birth, but time after time this fact is denied by the names of Hanseats occurring in the documents, as the above-mentioned Servoise Gomans.

" The Communinalty complained that John de Rous, Henry Coupman, Teostardus le Estreys, Ecbryth de Werle, Ralph de Alterderne, Henry Hoppe, Hard-moth and Hylderbraund, merchants of Almaine, received foreigners and traded with them, and although they were freed of customs for goods coming from their own parts of Almaine, they had become whole-sale merchants (grossoirs) in averdepoys, drapers and wool men and had meddled with merchandise be-longing to these trades without paying custom, and thus the Sherifs were defrauded of their customs. The defendants claimed freedom from tolls on all goods of this kind whencesoever they came. A day was given for them to argue their claim, and a jury summoned on the other charges against them." [1]

" Ralph de Abbehale, draper of London, was attached to answer John de Boclaud, Knight, in a plea for trespass, where the latter complained that, having bought cloth to the value of £63.4. – from defendant, he gave him certain pledges for payment viz :—one guilded coylter, three garnaments, one hood of medley, two super-tunics furred with bys,[2] one coat and one hood furred with miniver,[3] six and a quarter ells of medley cloth and one serge value ten pounds, and the defendant had neither delivered the cloth nor returned

[1] Callendar of Early Mayor's Court Rolls.
[2] Bys, Bis, Buisses = the back of squirrel in winter. (Author's note.)
[3] Miniver = belly of squirrel in winter. (Author's note.)

the pledges. The latter admitted the sale, and the pledges, but pleaded an agreement that, if the purchase price was not paid on a certain date he should require the pledges and he produced an unsealed deed to that effect. The plaintiff denied such an agreement and declared that the deed was none of his making, whereupon the defendant offered to produce at his own risk witnesses who were present in Thamys street at the handing over of the pledges." [1]

Evidently the Hansa were loath to deliver goods without payment even when such pledges were given. In fact, all through their history they were noted for their insistence on either cash down, or a level exchange.

The following letter from the reign of Edward III shows how close a watch they kept on the interests of their members, and what influence they could bring to bear to see their wrongs righted :

" Certifying that whereas Henry Ilyngham, a merchant of the Hanse of Almaine, had lately shipped two barrels of greywerk [2] at Bruges, on board a ship whereof Laurence Peresonne was master ; and the said ship had perished, and of the two barrels of greywerk one had been found in his seignory, and detained at Wrak, in the belief that all on board had perished. Evidence had been brought to show that the said barrels of grey werk were the property of Henry Ilyngham, and that none on board that ship had perished. He is asked to believe this testomony and to return to the said Henry or his atorney, the aforesaid barrel.

" The Holy spirit have him ever in his keeping,
" London, 26th January,
" Edward III (A.D. 1362/3)." [3]

[1] Callendar of Early Mayor's Court Rolls.
[2] Greywerk = badger fur. (Author's note.)
[3] Callendar of Letters from the Mayor and Corporation of London.

" Richard Spink and Thomas Halywell, skinners, and Thomas Luckford and William Horsecroft, discovered in the cellar of Henry Hydynghous, of the company of the Teutons of the Hanse, certain bellies of bievre [1] which were deceitfully mixed with false bellies, whereas, according to custom, such skins for sale should be entire and not cut, and all bellies without backs, the said Henry had offered for sale in the Ropery [2] certain bundles in which half bellies (mediventre) were mixed with whole bellies to the deceipt of the purchaser."

This charge was dismissed with half compensation as the defendant persisted that the buyer knew that some of the skins were only halves.

There is documentary evidence that the Aldermen of the Steelyard were very careful to keep on the right side of the Civic and Custom authorities, and many a good pair of gloves, wrapped round a nice sum in rose nobles, was sent to the head of the Customs, and many a keg of Rhenish, and fine barrel of caviare, sturgeon and smoked salmon, found their way into the cellars of the City Aldermen.

[1] Bievre = beaver. (Author's note.)
[2] The Ropery in Thames Street, so called because ropes were made and sold in that district. (Author's note.)

BERGEN KONTOR SEAL, 1754

PART III
DECLINE OF THE HANSEATIC LEAGUE

CHAPTER XV

EARLY CAUSES OF THE DECLINE OF THE HANSEATIC LEAGUE—FAILURE IN RUSSIA—LÜBECK'S WARS WITH THE DUTCH—THE LOSS OF LIVONIA AND BORNHOLM

IT must always be held in mind that the Hanseatic League did not decline suddenly throughout its entire organization. Its fall, like its rise, was gradual, and was achieved at a much earlier date in some countries than in others. For instance, the power of the League in the Steelyard persisted long after it had lost its Kontors at Novgorod, Bergen and Bruges, as well as its monopoly of trade throughout Scandinavia and the Baltic.

The League troubles in North-east Europe began with the rising in Prussia against the Order of Teutonic Knights. This war seriously interfered with their overland trade to Russia, and when, in 1466, the Treaty of Thorn forced the Teutonic Knights to give up the whole of West Prussia to Poland the League lost the allegiance of the Vistula cities.

The Hanseatic League do not seem to have realized until too late the danger that threatened them with the loss of Latvia and the neighbouring provinces, a mistake that was to cost them dear in loss of money, trade and prestige.

This blow was followed by a still more definite

disaster. Their harsh and autocratic behaviour in Russia had brought them into disfavour with Ivan III, and, in 1478, they were expelled from their famous old Kontor of St. Petershof in Novgorod. They managed to keep up a certain amount of trade with Russia for about another century and established small depots at Narva, Pleskov, Reval and Riga ; but, from the day the English discovered the sea route to Archangel, the end of the Hanseatic League in Russia was a foregone conclusion.

Little by little the League found themselves threatened on all sides. Denmark, Norway and Sweden began to grow restive under the unjust rule of these German merchants, who denied them even the right to fish in their own Baltic, and tried, in every possible way, to shut them out from all participation in the lucrative herring fisheries.

After the Treaty of Stralsund, the Hansa had had a great deal to say in the choosing of Danish Kings, and the League had always profited by the frequent quarrels between the three countries, to make use of their favourite tactics of playing off one monarch against the other. Now, various causes combined to bring about a failure of the Hanseatic League to maintain its supremacy in the Baltic.

One of these was the rapid rise of the Dutch. Round about 1425 the herrings left the Baltic waters off Scånia and Pomerania, and took to spawning in the North Sea, off the coast of Holland. This naturally removed a great deal of trade from the Baltic, where the Hansa were masters, and led to a marked increase in the wealth and power of Holland.

The Dutch had no love for the League, who had shut their fishermen out of the Baltic and who had always denied them any share in the carrying trade. Now, with their growing power, they were in a better position to defy the Hansa.

Their first step was to endeavour to make themselves of use to the ruling powers, thus undermining the influence of the Hanseatic League. For a time they were unsuccessful; but, on the accession to the throne of Germany of Charles V, King of Spain and the Netherlands, their opportunity arrived.

Charles was no friend of the insolent League of Cities who had usurped all too great a power throughout his new Empire, and who had closed the Baltic to his other subjects.

With one enemy on the throne of Germany and the Netherlands, the League was faced with another bitter opponent when Kristian II came to the throne of Denmark. As King of Norway, Kristian had already seen something of the Hansa tactics in Bergen, and had conceived no liking for the arrogant Germans. On his accession to the throne Kristian felt himself in no position openly to challenge the might of the League, in addition to which he wanted their help in the war that was already being waged between his country and Sweden; so, in return for their promise of assistance, he confirmed all their ancient rights and privileges.

Kristian was successful in his campaign against Sweden, and took Gustav Vasa prisoner. He was a harsh and brutal man, and subjected the young king to every indignity, till in 1519 the latter managed to escape from the Danes and took refuge in the free city of Lübeck, where he asked the civic authorities for protection. The city received him in a most friendly spirit, and for nearly a year he lived in the Kohlmarkt with a famous privateersman, one Kurt König.

Kristian ordered the city to send back Gustav Vasa, but the civic authorities, who were also heads of the Hanseatic League, had already realized that a united Scandinavia under Kristian II would mean the end of their power in the Baltic, and they had decided to give Gustav every assistance in regaining the crown of Sweden. So they refused to give him up, upon which Kristian, who was enraged at their defiance, asked the help of the Emperor Charles, complaining that the Hansa had closed the Baltic to all outsiders, and had absolutely refused to pay any tolls to Denmark.

The Emperor, who had already had trouble enough with the free cities, supported Kristian, and ordered Lübeck to give up Gustav ; but Lübeck persisted in her defiance of Kristian, and gave every assistance to Gustav Vasa, who in the meantime had returned to Sweden and was busy establishing himself in his own country with the help of his famous army of Dalecarlian peasants, and the considerable amounts of money supplied him by Lübeck.

Kristian continued his struggle against Gustav Vasa and the League, and in the meantime all trade between the Hansa and Denmark was at a standstill. During this campaign Kristian showed all the treachery and faithlessness that were such marked characteristics of his nature, and which were to bring him into strong disfavour with Charles V. He endeavoured to trick Charles into giving him the " insignificant little port of Lübeck " ; but, by a fortunate chance, Charles was better informed as to the size of the city, and refused.

In the midst of his war with Sweden, Kristian found himself faced with grave internal revolts in his own land, till at last he was forced to give up all his grand ideas of conquering Sweden and getting the better of Lübeck, and was compelled to flee the country.

In 1523, largely through the influence of the Hanseatic League, Frederick I of Holstein was placed on the throne of Denmark. In return for their assistance the League demanded his help against the Dutch.

It was significant of the growing lack of unity among the cities that Hamburg, Rostock and Lüneburg refused to take any part in a war against the Dutch.

Thus the League was instrumental in setting Gustav Vasa on the throne of Sweden, and Frederick I on that of Denmark, and in return for their assistance they were given a renewal of all their old privileges in Denmark and Sweden, and a fifty years' lease of the island of Bornholm.

This was a feather in the cap of Lübeck, and the League expected great things from Scandinavia ; but it was to prove only a transitory success.

The menace in the Baltic still persisted, and grew graver every year. The herrings had deserted it for the North Sea, the arrogance of the English merchants was increasing, while the Dutch were seizing a larger and larger share of the carrying trade ; added to which both the new Scandinavian Kings were to turn out a sad disappointment to the League.

Frederick promptly forgot the help he had received ; ignoring the promise he had given to Lübeck, he refused to allow them to continue their monopoly, or to insist on the exclusion of the Dutch from the Baltic, and he claimed equal rights for his own subjects. He even turned his unwelcome attention to Bornholm, where the Danes were complaining of their harsh treatment by the Germans.

By this time Gustav Vasa was firmly established on the throne of Sweden, and he was a king who had the good of his people for ever in his mind.

Despite all the kindness he had received from Lübeck, and the help the city had given him towards regaining his kingdom, he saw plainly enough how unjust and detrimental towards his subjects was the Hansa monopoly of the Baltic trade, and their privileged position in the Swedish cities. Even while availing himself of their assistance, he registered a vow to get rid of the Hanseatic League, as soon as the time was ripe.

In the early part of his reign he was prevented from carrying out his plan by the fact that he still owed large sums to the League, but, once secure on his throne, he started gathering together money, and paid off part of his debt. By 1527 Gustav was freely voicing his determination to rid Sweden of the Hanseats, and open his cities to other foreign merchants.

In vain did Lübeck try to use the King's debt to her as a lever with which to exert pressure in her favour ; Gustav went on collecting money with which to pay off the city ; no tax, however paltry, was overlooked in his desire to be free from all obligation to the League, and to escape from the domination of the Hansa.

The King was successful in his plans, and on his death, in 1560, Sweden found herself freed from the century-old tyranny of the Hansa.

In 1533, Frederick of Holstein died, and the Danes, encouraged by the example of Gustav Vasa, joined with Sweden in an anti-Hanseatic alliance. This alliance was to have a far-reaching effect on the history of Lübeck, for once again her rulers plunged her in a series of expensive and futile wars which left the Hanseatic League in a worse position than ever.

Gone was the unity of the League under such famous diplomats as Murmeister and Johan Pleskow, and no longer did the cities render such loyal and unquestioning obedience to their leaders.

After the death of Frederick, the League began to hope once more that they could now re-establish their power in the Baltic, and these hopes were fostered by a new leader who had risen in the Lübeck Senate.

Jurgen Wullenweber, later to become so famous in the annals of the city, was born in Hamburg, in 1492. He was the son of an unimportant merchant. Wullenweber, a man of fine honesty and burning with enthusiasm, had three causes dear to his heart : the betterment of the lower and middle classes, the re-establishment of the Hanseatic League in its old proud position, and the advancement of Lutheranism.

One of the prominent causes of unrest among the League Cities was the religious question, which had begun with the Reformation, and grown ever more serious.

While the Senate at Lübeck maintained the city's loyalty to the Catholic Religion, there was a large party among the lower classes who were anxious to see Protestantism established. In many of the League cities—among them Hamburg, Rostock, Stralsund, Wismar and Brunswick—the faith of Luther had already been adopted, and a bishop had been appointed for the Lutheran League Cities.

In Jurgen Wullenweber, the Protestants in Lübeck found a leader. The people, tired of the constantly levied tolls for the Lübeck wars, and incensed by the repeated refusals of the Senate to allow them to practise the Protestant Religion in peace, rose against the Civic authorities. This led to two parties in the Senate : the autocratic old régime led by Brömse, and the Protestant democratic party led by Wullenweber, who had been elected to the Senate. The result was that the Senate were compelled to allow the introduction of Protestantism into Lübeck.

At the time when the Hansa were hoping to regain their old power in the Baltic, Wullenweber was elected burgomaster. His first act was to call together a council before whom he placed his scheme. It was to arm a fleet and wipe the Dutch from the seas, thus seizing by force the command of the Baltic, just as they had done in the days of Valdemar Atterdag, before the Treaty of Stralsund ; thus at one blow re-placing the Hansa in their old position.

Wullenweber was a splendid orator, and his enthu-siasm won over the whole of the Senate. Lübeck decided to go to war with the Dutch for the mastery of the Baltic, and, having appealed in vain to Sweden and to the other League Cities to help her, she decided to carry out her plans herself. Wullenweber proceeded to collect money for the campaign and also to look about for a suitable commander. His choice fell on a certain Marx Meyer, also a native of Hamburg, and a man who had already made a name for himself as a bold and successful soldier of fortune.

Meyer was a romantic figure, and was to live for many years in German song and legend. Although a man of humble birth—he had begun life as a black-smith—he was possessed of great personal charm, and was destined to become the friend and favourite of a King, and the unhappy pawn of fortune.

So Meyer was given the command of the Lübeck fleet, and sailed away to fight the Dutch for the supremacy of the seas, and the monopoly of the carrying trade.

During his campaign he chased a fleet of Dutch ships and captured them just off the coast of England ; but, unfortunately for Meyer, they were carrying English goods, and on his landing, presumably in search of food and water, he was seized by the English, who put him in the Tower.

The Alderman of the Steelyard exerted every faculty to have Meyer released, and at last, on his representation, he was brought before Henry VIII.

Like every one else, Henry immediately fell a victim to his charming personality, and proceeded to treat him with every sign of favour, finally knighting him and sending him back to Lübeck with a large sum of money for the help of that Protestant city.

In the meantime a Dutch fleet had entered the
Baltic and seized many Lübeck ships, and ravaged
the towns on Scånia and Falsterbo. Finally an effort
was made towards peace, and in 1534 a conference
was called at Hamburg with a view to deciding terms.
Wullenweber and Meyer represented the Protestant
party in the Lübeck Senate, while Brömse was sent
on behalf of the old Catholic régime.

Wullenweber, according to the old Hansa policy,
curtly demanded that the Dutch should cease from
visiting the Baltic ; but he was opposed by Brömse,
and it was clear that his party was no longer so
favourably looked upon in Lübeck. Brömse's dislike and jealousy of Wullenweber had produced an
inevitable split in the Lübeck Senate. The decision
of the Council was in favour of the Dutch, and they
were granted a term of four years' grace in which
they might trade unmolested in the Baltic.

Wullenweber returned to Lübeck to complain
bitterly of the disloyalty of Brömse and the other
senators, and hotly to denounce this un-Hanseatic
favouring of the Dutch. Then, still obsessed with his
desire to see the Hanseatic League back in its old
position of power, he evolved a fresh plan, which was
to reinstate Kristian II on the throne of a Protestant
Denmark—always in the hope that he would give the
Hansa back their monopoly of the Baltic. For a time
this put fresh life into the Lübeck struggle. As
Wullenweber had expected, the Lutheran cities of
Hamburg, Lüneburg, Rostock, Wismar and Stralsund
now joined Lübeck in her project.

The League chose Count Christian of Oldenburg,

to liberate and reinstate Kristian II. But the enthu-
siasm of the League Cities was to last but a short
time ; they soon tired of the war, and still more of
the repeated demands on their city coffers, and
finally they refused to support Lübeck with further
funds. To add to his difficulties Wullenweber was
to be sadly disappointed in his commander, as well as
in his cities. When the latter failed him, he appealed
for aid to all the Protestant monarchs, but the only
one to stand by him was Henry VIII, who sent him
a large sum of money. While the monarchs were
anxious for the spread of Protestantism they were all
too often personal enemies of Kristian II. Count
Christian turned out a traitor to Wullenweber and to
Lübeck. The idea of freeing Kristian II did not
appeal to him as much as his own plan, which was to
set himself upon the throne of Denmark. Without
any hesitation he deserted the cause of Lübeck and
began to scheme for his own ends.

During this period, whilst Wullenweber was out of
the city, the Lübeck Senate was rapidly coming under
the influence of Brömse, who worked against Wullenweber at every turn. Then, to add to Wullenweber's
troubles, Marx Meyer was captured by Swedish troops
who were supposed to be his allies.

All unconscious of Count Christian's treachery,
Wullenweber endeavoured to carry on his campaign ;
he landed with a force in Zeeland, but the Lübeck
troops met with disaster on every hand, despite the
fact that the redoubtable Meyer had escaped and taken
the field once more.

Poor Wullenweber, cheated by his commander,

failed by his League Cities, and plotted against in the Senate by Brömse, who accused him of all manner of crimes that he had never committed, returned in 1535, a failure, with no alternative but to resign his burgomastership.

That was the end of the Lübeck struggle, and in 1536 Marx Meyer, the friend and favourite of Henry VIII, was captured and executed by the Danes.

But still Wullenweber persisted, and sought help in vain from the dissatisfied city of Copenhagen, always buoyed up by promises of assistance from Henry VIII, till finally he was seized at Hamburg and cast into prison.

Henry VIII, always his friend, made every endeavour to get him set free, but without avail. He was subjected to the most terrible tortures, in order to make him confess crimes of which he had patently never been guilty, among them that of being an Anabaptist, and at last, in 1537, without even the shadow of a fair trial, he was condemned to be executed.

So he suffered the fate of that other famous burgomaster of Lübeck, Wittemborg, who had failed in his project during the League wars against Valdemar, and been beheaded.

After a long resistance on the part of Copenhagen, Kristian III was recognized as King of Denmark. On the submission of Lübeck he granted the League certain modified privileges throughout his country ; but Gustav Vasa absolutely refused to grant them any like privileges in Sweden.

Thus one of the League's last bids for fame and

power failed. Lübeck was shamed and impoverished, the other League Cities were dissatisfied with her management, and all thoughts of a Scandinavian monopoly were at an end.

Had the Cities loyally and whole-heartedly supported Wullenweber and his project, the Hansa might have got back all their former power as the sole masters of the Baltic, but there was disunion among the cities, and jealousy and treachery in the Lübeck Senate, and the scheme was foredoomed from its very commencement.

But this was not to be the end of Lübeck's troubles. During her wars with the Dutch, a tremendous blow had been struck at her Russian trade ; a blow that was to shake the already failing Hanseatic League to its very foundations.

Not content with harassing the Germans in the Baltic and the North Sea, the English had succeeded in opening up a sea route to Russia via Archangel, thereby doing away with the necessity of employing the Germans as middlemen for the overland transport of merchandise to Novgorod and the North.

Neither was this all, for Livonia, conscious of the failure of the League to maintain order and obedience throughout all its Cities, had defied the Hansa and started independent trade with Russia.

Meanwhile Ivan the Terrible, an avowed enemy of the Hansa, was casting envious eyes on the province. This was indeed a grave menace, as it threatened the League's northern Baltic ports. In fact all Europe was alive to the growing danger of the Muscovite Empire ; and their fears proved well founded, for

Ivan sent a force into Livonia which, weakened by internal dissension, made little resistance.

Narva, Reval and Dorpat were taken, and it was all too late when Livonia appealed to the League for assistance. The Hansa, exhausted and apathetic after the Lübeck wars, did not realize until too late the gravity of such a loss ; and, by 1560, Livonia had been divided up between Poland, Sweden and Denmark.

This loss of Livonia was to lead to yet another and final war for Lübeck. Upon the death of Gustav Vasa, the League had opened up negotiations with his successor Erik XIV, who was not averse to making a compact with the Hansa, and even went so far as to offer them a renewal of certain of their privileges throughout Sweden ; but, in return, he demanded equal rights for Swedish merchants in all League Cities and the freedom of the Baltic.

Naturally the heads of the Hanseatic organization refused, upon which Erik lodged a formal protest against their continuing to trade with Russia, and forbade them to cross the Gulf of Finland, basing his protest on the assertion that German trade with Russia only served to encourage the menace of the Muscovite Empire.

This incensed Lübeck to such a degree that, regardless of the disasters which had attended her last unsuccessful wars, she formed an alliance with Frederick II of Denmark, and declared war on Sweden.

Unsupported by the other League Cities, Lübeck still managed to acquit herself with some success ; but, in the end, lack of funds and the general disapproval of the rest of the League compelled her to give in.

Peace was made in 1570 between Lübeck, Denmark and Johan of Sweden, and Lübeck managed to extort a promise from Sweden of the payment of the remainder of Gustav Vasa's debts, and also permission to continue trade with Russia through Narva ; but once made, these promises were soon set aside, and Johan of Sweden raised renewed objections to the Hansa trade with Russia.

Added to this, Lübeck experienced trouble with Frederick II. Despite the fact that Lübeck had been his ally against Sweden, he failed to show any consideration whatever towards the Hansa.   He extracted heavy money penalties from those League Cities whose ships had been found aiding Sweden ; and, worse still, he began to favour the Danes in their policy of revolt against the German rule in the island of Bornholm. Finally he intimated his intention of withdrawing the island from the suzerainty of Lübeck on the expiration of the fifty years' lease given by his grandfather, Frederick I.

In vain did Lübeck, depleted of money, deserted by its fellow League Cities, and worn out by its protracted wars, appeal for a renewal of the lease. Frederick II ignored her claims to having put Frederick I on the throne of Denmark and thus being entitled to privileges in Bornholm.

Lübeck was beaten, and the Hanseatic leaders were no longer in any position to enforce what they considered their rights, with the result that in 1576 Bornholm was returned to the Danes.

The League still continued a certain amount of trade with Russia, but with the capture of Narva by the Swedes, in 1587, their position in the city became untenable. For a time, Lübeck, through the personal favour of Feodor Ivanovitch, retained privileges in Novgorod and Pleskov, but he utterly refused to recognize the other Hanseatic cities, so that the League as a whole derived little advantage from his attitude.

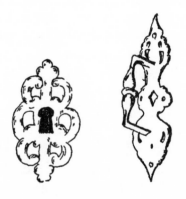

DOOR-FITTINGS

CHAPTER XVI

THE REMOVAL OF THE BRUGES KONTOR TO ANTWERP—
THE MERCHANT VENTURERS IN HAMBURG

WHILE Lübeck was waging her futile and almost single-handed wars, first against the Dutch, and then against the Swedes, the position of the League in Western Europe was growing steadily worse and worse.

With the loss of the Hanseatic monopolies and privileges in Russia, Scandinavia and the Baltic, it was only natural that the prestige of the League should suffer throughout its whole jurisdiction ; for it was upon these very monopolies and privileges that the power of the organization had been founded. Through this gradual but visible weakening, the loyalty of the Cities began to fail, and they rapidly became less united, some dropping out of the League altogether, while others rendered only a weak and intermittent obedience to Lübeck.

The Cities, led by Hamburg, which had always been jealous of Lübeck's position as head of the Hanseatic League, began to question the wisdom of the old League policy. All around them they saw non-Hanseatic Cities rising to power and riches through their unhindered trade with foreign merchants— principally the Dutch and the English—who year by year sent more traders all over Europe. By the most stringently enforced orders of the Hansa, her cities were forbidden to participate in this profitable trade; and this was one of the strongest causes of dissatisfaction among the League Cities.

In addition to the various troubles that were afflicting the League in Scandinavia and the Baltic, the famous old Kontor at Bruges had been practically ruined by the unhappy fate which overtook that city, when it came under the displeasure of the Emperor Frederick III. The ten years' blockade of Sluys, from 1488 onwards, almost put a stop to all trade with Bruges. But still the Hanseatic League might have been able to re-establish its trade in Bruges had it not been for their brutal, arrogant policy in the past, which had not endeared them to the Flemings, and had they been willing to offer reciprocal terms to the Netherland merchants. At last, when the position in Bruges became untenable, Lübeck decided on a momentous step : the Kontor was to be removed to another city. They were offered the choice of several towns, among them Amsterdam, which might have proved an excellent position, but Lübeck was still hostile to the Dutch, and had no desire to bring any increase of trade to one of their cities.

In 1545, they finally decided on Antwerp, which was rapidly rising in prosperity through the influx of foreign traders ; doubtless the Hansa thought that they would be able to deflect a goodly portion of this trade towards their own Kontor. Antwerp offered them excellent terms, but on the very aggravating condition that they should grant to the Antwerp merchants the same privileges in every League City as they enjoyed in Antwerp.

The fact that they accepted these terms shows how different was the position of the League now from a hundred years ago, when they would promptly have threatened to withdraw their favours, rather than share with foreigners a single one of their jealously guarded privileges. However, in 1564, the League began to build the great Hall of the Easterlings at Antwerp.

There was widespread dissatisfaction among the League Cities at this move on the part of Lübeck; and more especially did they object to the heavy tolls levied on their merchandise to cover the expenses of the new undertaking. There were also protests against the choice of Antwerp, and against the obstinacy of Lübeck in maintaining her policy of boycott towards all foreign merchants. Lübeck intimated her intention of running the new Antwerp Kontor on exactly the same lines as that of Bergen, with the same communal celibate life, and the same strict rules against fraternization and any attempt at independence.

This aroused a storm of protest from the individual merchants, who no longer cared to live the life of a monastic foundation in a civilized city like Antwerp.

The need of a Kontor, in the old sense of the word, had passed away ; and, with the advance of education and culture among the merchant classes, a desire had grown up for a greater independence in thought and action. They resented the heads of the organization in Lübeck dictating to them in every little pettifogging question concerning their business ; they often saw an opportunity for independent trade and were very loath to refuse it simply because the Hansa looked with disfavour upon the other party. But Lübeck persisted in her policy, with greater strictness than ever, and in 1568, the Antwerp Kontor was ready for occupation.

With all the old Hanseatic pomp it was handed over to the Alderman, Council and members; and so opened a phase of the Hanseatic League that was a failure before ever it began.

Even while the Kontor was being built, the League had found itself in money difficulties, for they had been unable to force the Cities to pay their dues, and the Hall of the Easterlings in Antwerp started its career heavily in debt.

The League made a great mistake in building a new and expensive Kontor in Antwerp. Their affairs were already in a bad state; and the troublous times in the Netherlands made trade difficult and unstable; added to which was the very evident difficulty of extorting money from the various cities for the running expenses of the Kontor.

Even now a change in policy might have saved them, for, had they given certain privileges to the foreign merchants, a large amount of trade would have been attracted to the Antwerp Kontor.

Then, to add to all the other causes of failure, there was the rising in the Netherlands against the cruelty and oppression of the Spaniards; besides being a great hindrance to trade, this involved the League in constantly recurring difficulties.

In the good old times the Hansa had been strong

enough to insist upon its neutrality, and could therefore derive benefits from both the warring parties,
but now the enfeebled League found itself at the
mercy of whichever party happened to be in power,
and had to abide by its decisions, and pay whatever
tolls it levied.

Both Philip of Spain and the Prince of Orange put
heavy import duties on all Hanseatic merchandise,
and the latter even went so far as to demand the
cessation of all trade with Spain. To make matters
worse, the League, faced with the ever-growing debts
of the Antwerp Kontor, levied such crippling taxes
on the merchandise from the various League Cities that
what trade there was was almost taxed out of existence.

While the League in the Netherlands was trying its
best to establish its Kontor in Antwerp, the Dutch
and, especially, the English were rapidly becoming
the masters of the sea trade, and their merchants were
extending their activities in every direction.

Several of the League Cities began to cast envious
eyes at this lucrative trade which was forbidden them
by the Hanseatic League. Hamburg had been the
first of the League Cities to rebel against the rulings
of Lübeck. Always jealous of that city for being
chosen head of the Hansa, Hamburg seized the opportunity, when Lübeck was faced with difficulties on
every side, to escape from her tyranny, and to lead a
certain number of the Cities against the old Hanseatic
régime.

Having refused to give Lübeck any assistance in
her war against the Dutch, Hamburg proceeded to
monopolize almost the whole of the Dutch trade that

had been deflected from the Baltic cities. In fact, for a time at least, Hamburg practically ceased to be a League City, although, at a later date, it was to join Lübeck and Bremen in an alliance that was to be the last faint shadow of the great Hanseatic League.

After opening up her markets to the Dutch, Hamburg was audacious enough to make a successful bid for a share in the English cloth trade. All dealings with the English had been expressly forbidden by the heads of the League, but, attracted by the ever-growing foreign trade, Hamburg ignored this command, and continued in her policy of defiance, with the result that by 1558, when Lübeck had impoverished herself by her long and futile wars, Hamburg was in a more flourishing position than ever before in its history.

With the rise of the Merchant Venturers, whom Sir Thomas Gresham had the impudence to call " the English Hansa," a steadily increasing stream of trade flowed into the Netherlands and Germany.

While in search of a depot, they settled in the non-Hanseatic City of Emden, the Netherlands being at that time closed to them on account of the war between Spain and Elizabeth. The founding of this depot led to a rapid rise in the prosperity and trade of Emden, a fact that was not lost upon the ruling powers of Hamburg, who, when in 1565 the English were compelled to leave Emden, came forward with an offer of a ten years' privilege in their city.

The Merchant Venturers accepted, and established their headquarters in Hamburg, which very naturally caused much jealousy and ill-feeling among the other League Cities.

The heads of the organization in Lübeck were furious at this unprecedented move on the part of Hamburg, and accused this city of disobedience and disloyalty ; but, although rather alarmed at the storm they had caused, Hamburg persisted in its independent policy, and for ten years the English merchants flourished there, to the great benefit of the trade of the city.

On the expiration of the ten years' lease, however, so great was the outcry made by the majority of the League Cities, and so bitter was the opposition of Lübeck, that Hamburg dared not renew it, and the Merchant Venturers left the city. However, they only removed to Stade, which served to increase Lübeck's anger, for the League had imagined that the Merchant Venturers would leave Germany altogether.

Needless to say, Hamburg was extremely sorry to see them go, and managed to maintain a certain portion of their trade, till, in 1611, with the power of the Hanseatic League growing weaker and weaker, the city decided that the English trade was worth more than the protection of a visibly weakening organization, and the English merchants returned to Hamburg never more to sever their connection with that city.

Hamburg also added considerably to its later prosperity by joining with several other League Cities in offering a home to the many fine craftsmen who were fleeing from the cruelty of the Spaniards in the Netherlands, and this far-sighted policy proved an excellent one, for these men established many a flourishing industry in the city. Lübeck strongly disapproved of this move also ; in fact, the heads of the organization seemed to have lost all foresight in their dealings with affairs in Europe.

So, while Hamburg prospered by the English and Dutch trade, the League were steadily losing their supremacy throughout Europe ; and, moreover, the new Kontor at Antwerp was proving an utter failure.

Many were the letters sent by the Hanseats of Antwerp to Lübeck complaining of the independent trade with foreigners that had been established by Hamburg and several of the League Cities. Hampered with debts in the very beginning of its career, and quite incapable of forcing the cities to pay their tolls and dues, the Kontor had never been able to get its head above water. To add to the troubles the members were proving obstinate and unruly. No longer could the Alderman and Council keep order within the Kontor ; and more and more disputes were taken to the courts of Antwerp, often with the result that the Hanseatic rulings were set aside.

At last Lübeck found herself powerless to render any aid to her members in Antwerp, and, crushed by internal and external forces working against it, the League had to stand by and see the vast, empty Hall of the Easterlings occupied by the Spanish forces, who entered it in 1624 and remained there for over twenty-five years.

Gone was the power and might of the Hanseatic League. The Kontors of Novgorod, Bergen and Bruges were closed, and the last white elephant at Antwerp had justified the prognostications of failure made by so many of the League Cities.

There still remained the Steelyard in London

where a more strongly united policy, and a certain lack of the disloyalty and insubordination that marked the internal life of the other Kontors had maintained the League in a better position than anywhere else in Europe.

But grave troubles were already threatening the Steelyard, and the day of the German merchants in England was rapidly drawing to a close ; and, with the fall of their last Kontor, the great trading organization of the Hanseatic League was to pass out of existence.

SEAL OF HAMBURG

CHAPTER XVII

TROUBLES IN ENGLAND—RISE OF THE MERCHANT VEN-
TURERS—DISCOVERY OF THE WHITE SEA ROUTE TO
ARCHANGEL—THE MUSCOVY COMPANY

WHILE the passing years found the power of
the Hanseatic League weakening throughout
Europe, their power and commerce in England was
not materially impaired until the middle of the six-
teenth century.

There had certainly been frequent disagreements
between the English and the Germans resulting in
correspondingly strained relations between the various
English Kings and the overlords of the Hanseatic
League ; but, annoying as these disturbances were,
the League had always managed to get their own way
in the end, and have all their old privileges confirmed.

The Germans had always claimed for themselves
alone the favourable terms of Edward III's Carta
Mercatoria, and compared with the status of the
German merchants that of other foreign traders in
England was extremely insignificant.

During the reign of Henry VIII, there had been
several contretemps between the Steelyard and that
irascible monarch ; but, on the whole, Henry was an
excellent friend to the Hansa, especially to the Protestant Cities who had joined the Smalkald Union.

In addition to sending considerable monetary help to Lübeck in her struggles against the Dutch, and doing all in his power to procure the release of Wullenweber, Henry confirmed and extended all the League privileges in England, and did his best to protect the members of the Steelyard against the growing jealousy of the English merchants.

During this period, Sir Thomas Gresham, always one of the most bitter and persistent enemies of the Hansa, was in Antwerp, managing various foreign affairs for the King. He lived for many years in that city, and it was due to his clever, if scarcely unimpeachable, financial tactics in 1551 that the value of the English pound was inflated on the Antwerp Bourse with such success that Edward VI escaped from his grave financial embarrassments and was able to pay off his very considerable debts without recourse to the Hansa. Undoubtedly Gresham's knowledge of trade conditions in Antwerp was of very great help to the Merchant Venturers in establishing their trade with the Netherlands.

Upon the death of Henry VIII, the Hanseatic League was to enter into a troubled phase in their life in England, a phase that was the precursor of the fall of the Steelyard.

At first Edward, the Boy King, confirmed all the Hanseatic privileges, but the commonalty of London, led by Sir Thomas Gresham, were persistent in their demands for justice against the hated Germans.

Gresham had the cause of the Merchant Venturers very near to his heart and never missed an opportunity of impressing upon Edward's Regent, the Duke of

Northumberland, the urgent necessity for restricting the privileges of the Hanseatic merchants. He was untiring in pointing out the many injustices that the English merchants had to put up with. They were constantly ill-treated by the German merchants abroad, who utterly ignored the reciprocity clause of the Treaty of Utrecht ; and in addition to this, the favourable Custom dues allowed to the Hanseatic merchants severely handicapped the English in their efforts to establish a lucrative trade with Europe. To add insult to injury, the Hansa were accused of taking bribes for smuggling into England the goods of non-Hanseatic merchants under the cloak of their ancient privileges, thus cheating the Treasury out of large sums of money in Custom duties.

Many a time before had the Lord Mayors of London placed these very same complaints before the reigning King, in the hope that they would be able to induce him to rescind the Hanseatic privileges ; but in the good old days the Kings often had need of the powerful Hanseatic League and were in no position to offend them ; but now the times had changed. Edward was under no obligation to the Hanseatic League and did not need their monetary assistance—Gresham was too clever a financial adviser for that—and, in addition, the English trade had now made such strides that it was beginning to be of great benefit to the Treasury. After a year or two Edward, taking the advice of his wise Councillors, began to alter his policy towards the Hanseatic League and, in 1552, after an inquiry into the differences of opinion between the Merchant Venturers and the Germans of the Steelyard, all the ancient privileges of the Hansa were declared forfeit and the German merchants were placed on the same footing as all the other foreign merchants trading with England.

This caused a certain amount of uneasiness in the Councils of the League, who hastened to send an ambassador over to England to plead for the restitution of their privileges. The heads of the organization did not imagine for one moment that the situation in England was as grave as it proved to be. The privileges had often been repealed, but, by their astute diplomacy, they had always managed, sooner or later, to get them renewed again.

Edward gave only an unsatisfactory answer to the ambassadors ; he allowed them certain modified privileges, but he made it very clear that he had every intention of protecting his own Merchant Venturers and doing everything in his power to further their trade.

To add to the League's troubles in England, the Steelyard began to be imbued with the same spirit of dissatisfaction that had arisen in the other Kontors. The members were gradually becoming more disloyal, and were revolting against the strict and obsolete Kontor Laws. Member after member was arraigned for breaking the law against independent trading, and there arose grave breaches in the honesty of the German merchants, an honesty that up to now had been the proud boast of the Hanseatic League in all its dealings.

In 1553, when the situation was beginning to look very grave indeed for the prospects of the League in England, Edward died and Mary came to the throne.

The Steelyard authorities made haste to greet the new Catholic Queen, with every sign of deference; and endeavoured to curry favour with the people of London by giving magnificent entertainments, with free food and wine, during the Coronation festivities; and—the usual clever and astute move—they placed considerable funds at the disposal of the new monarch.

The result was that one of Mary's first moves was to repeal the restrictions placed on the German merchants by Edward VI, and to renew all the ancient Hanseatic privileges. Once again the Hanseatic League was in its old proud position of first favourite in the English trading world.

In their eagerness to re-establish their old monopoly, the heads of the League even forgot a great deal of their recent Protestant fervour, a fact which did not add to their popularity among the Protestant League Cities.

This move on the part of Mary was deeply resented by the merchants of the City of London, who never for one moment desisted from their struggle for their rights.

Under the energetic guidance of Gresham, public opinion was rapidly turned against the Queen's policy; till at last complaints against the German merchants became so grave that she dare no longer ignore them.

And indeed there was every ground for dissatisfaction, for in 1554 the German merchants were exporting no less than forty-four thousand pieces of cloth out of England, while the English carried a paltry one thousand one hundred; in addition to which the Hanseats paid only one-tenth of the current export dues, for, under their privileges, they paid at the old rate of export dues, although these had been repeatedly raised.

The English trade was further injured by the fact that the Germans exported a large quantity of these cloths in an undyed condition, thus paying only the lowest rate of duty, and, by dyeing the cloth themselves, abroad, and selling it at a greatly increased price, they were able to undersell the English merchants in the foreign markets.

In 1554 the Privy Council examined the matters at variance between the Merchant Venturers and the merchants of the Hansa.

The Merchant Venturers alleged that the Hansa merchants living in London took English white cloth to Antwerp and sold it there to the hindrance of the English merchants, and that owing to their great success during the last few years they shipped more and more of this cloth to Antwerp and Hamburg, " intendinge as it seemeth to mayntayn a traffique and therby hinder the said merchants from their trade."

They also complained that the Hansa merchants " doe bringe into England great quantities of forryn waires not even made in their countrie. It is to be feared that they thereby meane to get all the traffique into their owne hands, and so let or overthrowe the Companie of the Merchants Adventurers."

The Hansa merchants called to answer these charges informed the Privy Council that they stood by the maintenance of their privileges, and alleged that they had done nothing but what they were allowed to do by those same privileges.

The decision taken by the Privy Council was that there should be a modification in the Hanseatic Privileges. They were forbidden " to shippe or transport out of this Realme any maner of cloothes into the Citie of Andwarp or any of the Emperor's Low Countries " ; and they were not to carry to other parts any greater number of white cloths than after the rate of one white to every three coloured.

If they contravened this order they were to pay subsidy on each cloth " like other strangers do pay."

Also, for every three pounds' value of goods brought into England from their own country, they were permitted to bring in only one pound's value of foreign goods (that is, goods not of German origin).

If they brought in more than the proportion of one-fourth of foreign goods they were to pay the same Custom dues on them as all the other foreign merchants paid.[1]

Thus the ancient privileges of the Hanseatic League were much curtailed, especially in their export of English cloth, which at one period brought them in over sixty thousand pounds yearly.

After making every effort to induce Mary to restore them to favour, the League had recourse to their old threat of ceasing to trade with England, but with the changed times this threat was but empty words.

A majority of the League Cities no longer rendered their old blind obedience to the Hanseatic orders ; and now they refused to close their doors to the extremely profitable English trade.

While the League was vainly trying to think of some

[1] Landsdowne 170, folio 155 (dated Feb. 25th, 1554).

scheme whereby it could get back its old monopoly in England, Mary died and was succeeded by Elizabeth.

In Elizabeth, the Hanseatic League were to meet their match at last. Her first thought was always for her own people and she was to prove a firm friend and ally to the Merchant Venturers.

In the whole history of English commerce there are no more colourful and romantic pages than those concerning the Company of Merchant Venturers.

The Merchant Venturers Company was a development of the early trade guilds, but its activities were far more widespread than those of other chartered companies such as the Merchants of the Staple.

With the vast improvement of the English ships, and the gradual opening up of fresh trade routes to the new world, a great impetus was given to the English merchants, an impetus that was fostered by the restrictions upon the Hanseatic trade in England and that was to reach its apogee during and following the reign of Elizabeth, when the Merchant Venturers were employing fifty thousand persons in the Netherlands alone, and doing a trade with the Netherlands and Germany that in the reign of James I was worth a million a year.

The Dutch, French and Russian nations were only too willing to grant charters to foreign merchants, and this period was to see the founding of the Muscovy Company, the Levant Company and the Eastland Company, apart from other charters granted to Companies trading with the Indies and the rest of the newly discovered world.

The Muscovy Company was one of the most fatal

rivals of the Hanseatic League and led directly to its downfall in Europe.

In 1550, Sebastian Cabot had received two hundred pounds for his services in restricting the English trade of the Hanseatic League and for his help in establishing the Company of Merchant Venturers. It was under his auspices, as Governor of the Merchant Venturers, that, in May, 1553, the Company equipped three ships —the " Bona Esperenza," the " Edward Bonaventure " and the " Bona Confidentia "—under Sir Hugh Willoughby and Richard Chanceler, to make an attempt to reach China by the North-East Sea route.

During a gale the ships were separated, Willoughby and his men were obliged to winter on the icy coast and perished. But Chanceler, with Stephen Boroughs, his navigator, in the " Edward Bonaventure," rounded a headland they named the North Cape, and sailed up the White Sea to the Bay of St. Nicholas, afterwards the site of the town of Archangel.

Having waited for a time to see if the other ships joined them, Chanceler and his men proceeded on their voyage of discovery. The following description is taken from Hakluyt's *English Voyages* :

" To conclude, when they saw their desire and the hope of the arrivall of the rest of the shippes to be every day more and more frustrated, they provided to sea againe, and Master Chanceler held on his course towards that inknown part of the world, and sailed so farre, that hee came at last to the place where hee found no night at all, but a continuall light and brightnesse of the Sunne shining clearly upon the huge and mightie Sea. And having the benefite of this perpetuall light for certaine dayes, at the length it pleased God to bring them into a certaine great Bay, which was one hundred miles or thereabouts over. Whereinto they entered, and somewhat farre within it cast ancre, and looking every way about them, it happened that they espied a farre off a certaine fisher boate, which Master Chanceler, accompanied with a fewe of his men, went towards to common with the fishermen that were in it, and to knowe of them what Countrey it was, and what people, and of what manner of living they were ; But they being amazed with the strange greatnesse of his shippe, (for in those partes before that time they had never seene the like) beganne presently to avoyde and to flee ; but hee still following them at last overtooke them, and being come to them, they (being in great feare, as men halfe dead) prostrated themselves before him, offering to kisse his feete ; but hee (according to his great and singular courtesie) looked pleasantly upon them, comforting them by signes and gestures, refusing those dueties and reverences of theirs, and taking them up in all loving sort from the ground. And it is strange to consider howe much favour afterwards in that place, this humanitie of his did purchase to himselfe. For they being dismissed spread by and by a report abroad of the arrival of a strange nation, of a singular gentlenesse and courtesie ; whereupon the common people came together offering to these new-come ghests victuals freely, and not refusing to traffique with them, except they had beene bound by a certaine religious custome, not to buy any forreine commodities, without the knowledge and consent of the king.

" By this time our men had learned that this Countrey was called Russia, or Moscovie, and that Ivan Vasiliwich (which was at that time their King's name) ruled and governed farre and wide in those places. And the barbarous Russes asked likewise of our men whence they were, and what they came for ;

whereunto answere was made, that they were Englishmen sent into those coasts, from the most excellent
King Edward the sixt, having from him in commandement certaine things to deliver to their King, and
seeking nothing els but his amitie and friendship, and
traffique with his people, whereby they doubted not,
but that great commoditie and profit would grow to
the subjects of both kingdomes.

" The Barbarians heard these things very gladly,
and promised their aide and furtherance to acquaint
their king out of hand with so honest and a reasonable
request.

" In the meantime Master Chanceler intreated
victuals for his money of the governour of that place
(who together with others came aboord him) and
required hostages of them likewise for the more
assurance of the safetie to himselfe and his company.
To whom the Governours answered, that they knew
not in that case the will of their king, but yet were
willing in such things as they might lawfully doe, to
please him ; which was as then to afford him the
benefit of victuals.

" Nowe while these things were adoing, they
secretly sent a messenger unto the Emperour, to
certifie him of the arrival of a strange nation, and
withall to knowe his pleasure concerning them.
Which message was very welcome unto him, insomuch
that vouluntarily hee invited them to come to his
Court. But if by reason of the tediousness of so long
a journey, they thought it not best so to doe, then hee
graunted libertie to his subjects to bargaine, and to
traffique with them ; and further promised, that if it
would please them to come to him, hee himselfe would
beare the whole charges of poste horses. In the
meantime the governours of the place differed the
matter from day to day, pretending divers excuses,
and saying one while that the consent of all the

govourners, and another while, that the great and waightie affaires of the kingdome compelled them to differ their answere ; and this they did of purpose, so long to protract the time, untill the messenger (sent before to the king) did returne with relation of his will and pleasure.

" But Master Chanceler, (seeing himself held in this suspence with long and vaine expectation, and thinking that of intention to delude him, they posted the matter off so often,) was very instant with them to performe their promise ; Which if they would not doe, hee tolde them that hee would depart and proceede in his voyage. So that the Moscovites (although as yet they knew not the minde of their king) yet fearing the departure in deede of our men who had such wares and commodities as they greatly desired, they at last resolved to furnish our people with all things necessarie, and to conduct them by land to the presence of their king. And so Master Chanceler beganne his journey, which was very long and most troublesome, wherein hee had the use of certaine sleds, which in that countrie are very common, for they are carried themselves upon sleds, and all their carriages are in the same sort, the people almost not knowing any other manner of carriage, the cause whereof is the exceeding hardnesse of the ground congealed in the winter time by the force of the colde, which in those places is very extreme and horrible, whereof hereafter we will say something.

" But nowe they having passed the greater part of their journie, mette at last with the Sleddeman (of whom I spake before) sent to the king secretly from the Justices or governours, who had by some ill happe lost his way, and had gone to the Sea side, which is neere to the countrie of the Tartars, thinking there to have found our ship. But having long erred and wandered out of his way, at the last in his direct retourne, hee met (as hee was coming) our Captaine on the way. To whom he by and by delivered the Emperours letters, which were written to him with all courtesie and in the most loving manner that could be ; wherein expresse commandement was given, that post horses should bee gotten for him and the rest of his companie without any money. Which thing was of all the Russes in the rest of their journey so willingly done, that they began to quarrell, yea, and to fight also in striving and contending which of them should put their post horses to the sledde ; so that after much adoe and great paines taken in this long and wearie journey, (for they had travailed very neere fifteene hundred miles) Master Chanceler came at last to Mosco, the chiefe citie of the kingdome, and the seate of the king ; of which citie, and of the Emperour himselfe, and of the principall cities of Moscovie, wee will speake immediately more at large in this discourse." [1]

Thus was the White Sea route to Russia made known to the English. It is quite erroneous to say that it was " discovered " by the English, as it was already well known to the Norwegian traders.

Chanceler managed to make his way to Moscow, where he presented Edward's letters to the Emperor and made arrangements for the opening up of a possible trade with Russia. As will be seen from the following account, the Hanseats at Novgorod strongly resented the presence of the English in Russia and did everything in their power to prejudice the Emperor against them ; but by now they were powerless to hinder the spread of English trade :

[1] *The Principal Voyages of the English Nation*, Hakluyt, Vol. I, pp. 274-7. (Everyman Edition.)

" Next unto Mosco, the Citie of Novogorode is reputed the chiefest of Russia ; for although it be in Majestie inferior to it, yet in greatnesse it goeth beyond it.   It is the chiefest and greatest Marte Towne of all Moscovie ; and albeit the Emperours seate is not there but at Mosco, yet the commodiousnesse of the river, falling into that gulfe which is called Sinus Finnicus, whereby it is well frequented by Marchants, makes it more famous than Mosco it selfe.   This town excells all the rest in the commodities of flaxe and hempe ; it yeeldes also hides, honie and waxe. The Flemings there sometimes had a house of Marchandize, but by reason that they used the like ill dealing there, which they did with us, they lost their privileges, a restitution whereof they earnestly sued for at the time that our men were there.   But those Flemings hearing of the arrivale of our men in those parts, wrote letters to the Emperour against them, accusing them for pirats and rovers, wishing him to detaine and imprison them.   Which things when they were knowen of our men, they conceived feare, that they should never have returned home.   But the Emperour beleeving rather the Kings letters, which our men brought, then the lying and false suggestions of the Flemings, used no ill intreatie towards them." [1]

The following is an account of Chanceler's journey by land from Archangel to Moscow in which he tells of the various towns through which he passed, and the goods to be found there :

" Russia is very plentiful both of land and people, and also welthy for such commodities as they have. They be very great fishers for Salmons and small coddes ; they have much oyle which wee call treine

---

[1] *The Principal Voyages of the English Nation*, Hakluyt, Vol. I, p. 285. (Everyman Edition.)

oyle, the most whereof is made by a river called Duina.
They make it in other places but not so much as there.
They have also a great trade in seething of salte water.
To the north part of that countrey are the places
where they have their Furres, as Sables, marterns,
greese Bevers, Foxes white, blacke, and redde, Minkes,
Ermines, Miniver and Harts. There are also fishes
teeth, which fish is called a Morsse. The takers
thereof dwell in a place called Postesora, which bring
them upon Hartes [1] to Lampas to sell, and from
Lampas carie them to a place called Colmogro, where
the hie market is holden on Saint Nicholas day. To
the west of Colmogro there is a place called Gratanove,
in our language Novogorode, where much fine Flaxe
and Hempe groweth, and also much waxe and honie.
The Dutch marchants have a Staplehouse there.
There is also great store of hides and at a place called
Plesco ; and thereabout is great store of Flaxe, Hempe,
Waxe, Honie ; and that town is from Colmogro 120
miles.

" There is a place called Vologda ; the commodities
whereof are Tallowe, Waxe and Flaxe ; but not so
great plenty as is in Gratanove. From Vologda to
Colmogro there runneth a river called Duyna, and
from thence it falleth into the sea. Colmogro serveth
Gratanove, Vologda and the Mosco with all the
country thereabout with salte and saltfish. From
Vologda to Jeraslave is two hundred miles ; which
towne is very great. The commodities thereof are
hides, and tallowe, and corne in great plentie and some
Waxe, but not so plentiful as in other places.

" The Mosco is from Jeraslave two hundred miles.
The countrey betwixt them is very wel replenished
with small villages, which are so well filled with people,
that it is wonder to see them ; the ground is well
stored with corne which they carrie to the citie of

[1] Reindeer. (Author's note.)

Mosco in such abundance that it is wonder to see it. You shall meete in a morning seven or eight hundred sleds coming or going thither, that carry corne and some carie fish. You shall have some that carie corne to the Mosco, and some that fetch corne from thence, that at the least dwell a thousand miles off ; and all their cariage is on sleds. Those which come so farre dwell in the north partes of the Dukes Dominions, where the cold will suffer no corne to grow, it is so extreme. They bring thither fishes, furres, and beastes skinnes. In those parts they have but small store of cattell.

"The Mosco itself is great ; I take the whole towne to bee greater than London with the suburbes ; but it is very rude, and standeth without all order. Their houses are all of timber very dangerous for fire. There is a faire Castle, the walls whereof are bricke and very high ; they say they are eighteene foote thicke, but I doe not beleeve it, it doeth not so seeme, notwithstanding I doe not certainely knowe it ; for no stranger may come to view it. The one side is ditched and on the other side runneth a river called Moscua which runneth into Tartarie and so into the sea called Mare Caspium ; and on the north side there is a base towne, the which hath also a bricke wall about it, and so it joyneth with the Castle wall. The Emperor lieth in the castle, wherein are nine fayre Churches, and therein are religious men. Also there is a Metropolitane with divers Bishops. I will not stande in description of their buildings nor of the strength thereof because we have better in all points in England. They be well furnished with ordinance of all sortes." [1]

On his return voyage Chanceler's vessel was seized

[1] *The Principal Voyages of the English Nation*, Hakluyt, Vol. I, pp. 254, 255, 256. (Everyman Edition.)

by some ships belonging to the Hansa, but he managed
to escape and arrived safely in London with his letters
from the Emperor. The latter expressed his willing-
ness to grant Edward's request for trading facilities,
and to accord to the English merchants to go and
come, and attend all fairs and markets where they
might sell their goods and buy Russian merchandise
for transport into England. The Emperor also granted
to the English to take ships to Russia whenever they
pleased and in whatever numbers.

This expedition of Chanceler's laid the foundation
for the famous Muscovy Company that was to deal
the final death-blow to the already failing trade of the
Hanseatic League in Russia.

In 1555 the Merchant Venturers were granted a
Charter for their Muscovy Company for the furtherance of trade between England and Russia, and for
the discovery of further trade routes through Russia
with a view to opening up commerce with the adjoining
lands.

The following is a brief outline of the first privileges
granted to the Merchant Venturers of the Muscovy
Company. The Emperor guaranteed:

(1) Safe conduct throughout his realms for all
members, of whatever ranks of the Merchant Venturers
of the Muscovy Company, with full liberty and
freedom to journey by sea, land or water to whatsoever
place they chose, there to sojourn in pursuance of their
business, without any restraint, or the enforcement of
any toll, due or custom on their ships or wares. The
said merchants to be under no fear of distraint on their
wares.

(2) That the Company were free to choose their own agents, clerks, packers, carriers and porters for the buying, weighing, measuring and transporting of their merchandise with leave to punish or dismiss the same for any disobedience or breach of their regulations.

(3) That he would recognize a chosen head of the Muscovy Company in Russia and allow him absolute freedom in governing the English members and in administering justice in all their disputes.

(4) In the case of any member rebelling against the orders of the Company the Emperor promised the help of the Russian authorities in bringing him to justice, and to this end the Company were to be allowed the free use of any Russian prisons.

(5) That justice should be expeditiously accorded to any Englishman appearing in the courts of the land. If the case came up for judgment during the absence of the Englishman, he was granted the right to appoint an attorney to conduct his case for him.

(6) That the Russian authorities would take every care that justice was done to any Englishman who should have been injured or cheated by a Russian subject. In the event of a member of the Company committing a punishable crime his merchandise should not be open to seizure ; and if a member were seized for a debt he should not be thrown into prison if he could provide satisfactory sureties from among the members of the Company.

(7) In all cases of piracy within the domain of Russia all steps should be taken to see justice done and the injured parties indemnified.

The founding of this Company came as a terrible blow to the Hanseatic League, for it threatened both their Russian and their carrying trade, but by this time the English were too firmly established for the League to be able to oust them.

Chanceler's expedition was followed by a second in 1556 when Boroughs, in the " Searchthrift," reached Nova Zembla ; and by a third in 1561 when Elizabeth addressed a letter to the Emperor of Russia asking for a safe-conduct for Anthony Jenkinson to pass through Russia on an embassy to the " Sophie of Persia."

LANTERN

CHAPTER XVIII

ELIZABETH AND THE HANSEATIC LEAGUE—THE FALL OF
THE STEELYARD—THE POLICY OF KING JAMES I

ON the accession of Queen Elizabeth, the Hanseatic League hastened to send their ambassadors with the usual flowery messages of congratulation; while, at the same time, they congratulated themselves upon having a woman to deal with, assuming that they would be able either to cajole, or bully her into renewing all the privileges rescinded by Edward VI.

But they were to be sadly disappointed. Certainly Elizabeth received their representatives with every outward mark of courtesy, but at the same time she showed them quite clearly that her first thought would be for her own Merchant Venturers and that she would do everything in her power to see justice accorded them, both at home and abroad.

With the discovery of the White Sea route to Russia a great impetus had been given to the trade of the Merchant Venturers, and Elizabeth's advisers, Sir Thomas Gresham and Lord Burghley, never ceased to impress upon her the serious damage that was being done to the English trade by the favoured German monopolists in their midst.

So, while still offering to give them certain advantages among the foreign merchants in London,

Elizabeth refused to give them back all the privileges they previously enjoyed, while in addition she demanded that the affairs of the Steelyard should be open to examination by the civic authorities of the city—a demand that was contrary to all principles of Hanseatic secrecy. At the same time the Queen insisted upon equal terms for her merchants in Germany, basing her claim upon the reciprocity clause in the Treaty of Utrecht, a clause that had caused constant trouble between the English and the Germans, who persisted in ignoring it.

Naturally the League refused her demand, and even went so far as to get the Emperor to send a letter to the Queen protesting against her " immoderate demands " ; but though this letter was formally presented by the heads of the Steelyard it had no effect whatever upon Elizabeth.

She was merely biding her time, at present she did not feel strong enough to turn the Hanseats out of England, so she let them remain ; but she increased their Customs dues, and severely cut down their allowance of wool for export, with the result that English trade prospered and spread.

The Germans countered by putting an embargo upon English trade abroad, but this was rendered null and void because several of the cities, led by Hamburg, had already opened their gates to the English Merchant Venturers. When at the expiration of the ten years' lease granted by Hamburg to the Merchant Venturers, the League were able to bring such pressure to bear that the city had reluctantly to see them depart to Stade ; and, after the Emperor Maximilian had been induced to forbid any German town to trade with the English without the permission of the Hanseatic League, Elizabeth still refused to restore the Hanseats to favour.   That she took no further steps to get rid of the Germans was doubtless due to her fear of losing the excellent ground that had been gained in several of the more important German cities.   She certainly put no trust in the League promises to allow the English merchants privileges in certain of their towns in return for the restitution of their full privileges in London.

For some years matters were at a standstill ; the League refusing to accede to Elizabeth's demands for fair treatment for her merchants abroad, while the Queen did not feel herself quite strong enough to expel them from England.

It was all in vain that the wise authorities of the Steelyard pointed out to Lübeck that trade in England had made such strides that it was impossible to demand their old privileges of monopoly, and it would be greatly to the advantage of the League to offer equal privileges to English merchants throughout Germany. Lübeck was obstinate in her refusal to give up a single one of her old advantages.

During this period the Steelyard was experiencing the same internal troubles that had undermined the powers of the other Kontors.   The members were more and more dissatisfied, they resented the petty, out-of-date rules and regulations and the upper ranks were indignant at Lübeck's constantly increasing demands for money.

They intimated to the heads of the League that they

were making barely enough money to cover the upkeep of the Steelyard and the other English depots
without having to send large sums abroad to bolster
up the tottering Kontor at Antwerp ; and finally they
utterly refused to supply Lübeck with further funds,
a refusal that would have called down dire penalties
in the old days of the League's supremacy.

Neither was the honesty of the Hanseats in England
as impeccable as it had been, and many were the
complaints of avoided tolls and smuggled goods
brought against the Steelyard by the citizens of
London.

Lübeck was at its wits' end, no longer could it
enforce its orders or restore unity among its cities, and
on every hand it was hard pressed to find sufficient
money to continue with its ambitious and short-
sighted policy ; yet it absolutely refused to give way
on any point that encroached upon its old-time
privileges.

In the Diet of 1590 Lübeck even went so far as to
demand from the cities their decision as to whether
they would remain under the Hanseatic League or not.
There was a half-hearted response led by Bremen
and Cologne, but it was evident that the Cities were
losing their faith in the League.

Meanwhile Elizabeth was awaiting her opportunity
in England, and it came with the vanquishing of the
Spanish Armada in 1588. Now the strength of the
English was assured and as masters of the sea they no
longer had any need for the Germans.

During the Spanish troubles the Hansa, sheltering
behind its neutrality, had driven a brisk trade in

carrying necessities to the Spaniards. Elizabeth protested to the Steelyard authorities against this breach
of faith, at which the League were extremely aggrieved
and made all their usual excuses ; but they were to be
still more aggrieved later on, for Elizabeth proceeded
to reprisals, and Drake seized sixty Hanseatic ships
laden with stores on their way to Spain.

The League made no secret of their annoyance ;
but it was all in vain, for they never got back a vestige
of those cargoes—Elizabeth had a way of keeping all
she laid her hands on.

In their annoyance the heads of the Hansa brought
further pressure to bear on the Emperor, with the
result that in 1597 he issued a belated proclamation
ordering all English merchants to leave his realm by
the end of three months and threatening, with the
severest penalties, any town that continued to harbour
the Merchant Venturers. By this step Lübeck hoped
to crush her hated rivals and undoubtedly expected
that they would give up all ideas of further trade with
Germany, and that Elizabeth would now be forced to
restore their privileges in order to keep her German
trade. But Lübeck had badly under-estimated both
Elizabeth's will and the secure position of English
trade ; the Queen was no woman to be forced into
submission by any League of German Merchants,
even if it had been in its hey-day, and not already
moribund.

The Merchant Venturers merely retired to Holland,
where they continued trading while they awaited
developments in England.

They had not long to wait. In 1598, enraged by a

further attempt on the part of the Hansa to interfere with the trade between Holland and England, Elizabeth took the decisive step that she and Lord Burghley had been keeping up their sleeves until they felt strong enough to make use of it.

She sent the following mandate to the Steelyard, ordering the Hanseats to leave within fourteen days :

"WARRANT v. THE STEELYARD

" Elizabeth, by the grace of God, Queen of England, Fraunce and Ireland, Defender of the Faith etc., To ye right trustie and welbeloved the Mayor and Sheriffs of our Citie of London greeting. Whereas there hath been directed a commandement by the name of a mandat from the Romaine Emperor to all Electors, prelates, Earles and all other offycers and Subjectes of the Empire, recyting sondrie complaintes made to him by the Allyed Townes of the Dutch Hanses in Germaine of dyvers iniuries committed against them in our Realme And lykewise uppon complaint made by them against the Companie of our marchauntes Adventurers without hearing of anie Aunsweare to be made to the said Hanse Townes in disproofe of theire complaintes, the same being most notoriously unjust, and not to be mainteyned by anie truthe ; And yet nevertheless by that mandat our English marchantes namely the Companie of Marchants Adventurers are forbidden to use and trafficque of marchaundize within the Empyre. But are commaunded to depart from thence uppon great paynes and to forbeare openly and secretly from all havens or landing places, or to use anie commerce by water or by land in the Empire, uppon payne of apprehension of their persons, and confiscation of theire goods, with sondry other extreame sentences pronounced against our saide subictes. Hereupon although we have sent expressely our letters

as well to the Emperor as to the Electors and princes
of the Empyre, declaring our opynion of this proceeding to be iniuriously prosecuted by the said Hanse
Townes and therefore have requyred to have the same
mandat either revoked or supperseded yet being un-
certaine what shall followe thereuppon. We have
thought it agreable for our honnor in the meane tyme
to commaund that all such as are here within our
Realme appertayning to the said Hanse Townes
situated in the Empire, and specially all such as have
residence within our Citie of London, either in the
House, comonly called the Stillyard or in anie other
place elsewheare, doe forbeare to use anie maner of
trafficque in way of merchaundise or to make anie
contracte, and likewise doe depart out of our domynions
in like sort as our subiectes are commaunded to depart
out of the Empyre, uppon like paynes, as are con-
tayned against our subiects in the said Mandat. And
for the execution of this our determynation we will
that you, the Mayor of our said Citie of London and the
Sheriffes shall forthwith repaire to the said House called
the Stillyard, and calling before you such as have the
charge thereof, or doe reside there, doe give them
knowledge of this our determynation and commandement, charging that by the eight and twentieth daie
of this month, being the daie, that our marchauntes
are to be anoyde from abroade, they doe depart out
of this our Realme, charging them also to give knowledge hereof to such, as be of anie the Hanse Townes
belonging to the Empire, remayning within anie part
of our Realme, to depart likewise by the said daie.
And you the Mayor and Sheriffes calling to you the
Offycers of our Customehouse, to take possession of
the said Howse, the said eight and twentieth daie, to
remaine in our Custodie untill we shall understande
of anie more favourable course taken by the Emperor
for restitutions of our Subjectes to their former law-

full trade within the Empire. And this shall be your warrant for the execution of the premisses.

"In Witness whereof our   (seal)

"(Ondosso 'This is required to passe immediately to the Great Seale' signed Burghly, Walsingham, Buckhurst.)" [1]

The Lord Mayor, with representatives of the commonalty, went in state to Thames Street and presented the order to the Alderman.

In the words of a member of the Steelyard :

"We left because it might not be otherwise ; heavy of heart, Alderman Heimrich Langermann led the way, and we followed him, and the gate was shut behind us, and we might nohow stay the night ! Heaven have pity on us !

"July 25.1598." [2]

So at last Burghley and Gresham had their way and the centuries old tyranny of the Hanseatic League in England was finally removed.

With what sorrow the head of the Steelyard must have led that pathetic procession of men out of the building that had been in the possession of German merchants since the tenth century ; the building that their pride and affection had ornamented and beautified, and whose walls had held their secrets through so many changing years.

The Germans had taught the English all they knew of business methods, and had established trade in England long before her people were proficient enough

[1] British Museum Manuscripts, Eg. 2603, F. 53.

[2] J. M. Lappenberg, *Urkundliche Geschichte des Hanschen zu London.*

to conduct their own affairs, but, as is so often the case, the pupils had outdistanced their masters, and having come into their own were now turning them out of the country. Still the Germans had enjoyed hundreds of years of a prosperous monopoly in England, and these years had been marked by arrogance and injustice ; they had persistently refused the English a share in their prosperity and were now merely reaping the reward of their unfair and short-sighted policy.

The Steelyard, though shorn of all its privileges, was to be returned to the Hanseatic League, and enjoy many more years of uneasy life in London.

After the expulsion from the Thames Street buildings, Elizabeth relented sufficiently to permit the Hanseats to remain in London, and the depots at Lynn and Boston were maintained for a modified trade. On the whole Elizabeth treated the Hanseats very well ; she did not distrain on any of their merchandise at the Steelyard and permitted them to sell off such as remained in store.

The Hanseatic League did not calmly accept this move on the part of the Queen ; nor did they give up all hopes of seeing their privileges restored at a future date. Their first move was to put an embargo on all English goods, but once more this was rendered nothing but an empty threat because various of the German Cities refused to obey, and continued their trade with England.

In 1602 the League arranged a meeting at Bremen between their ambassadors and envoys sent from England, at which they attempted to come to some decision concerning the troubles between them. The proceedings were long drawn out, and far from satisfactory, and it was not until 1603 that any real business was transacted. England refused to give way upon any of the points under discussion, and matters seemed at a deadlock when news came of the death of Elizabeth.

The League promptly broke off all negotiations. As usual their hopes rose at the thought of a new king who might be favourable to their cause.

Lübeck immediately made arrangements to send an embassage to James I, and representatives were chosen under the leadership of Krefting of Bremen, one of the cleverest diplomatists remaining to the League.

On this same journey Krefting was to visit Brussels to try and induce the Spanish governors to remove the crippling dues that had been put on Hanseatic goods ; and France, to endeavour to obtain a renewal of privileges that had recently been withdrawn.

By the express orders of Lübeck the ambassadors adopted the old insolent policy of insistence, and demanded the restitution of the Steelyard and the renewal of all their privileges, basing their demands on the ancient treaties, while at the same time they definitely refused any like privileges to the English merchants in Germany.

James did not treat the representatives of the League with any very great courtesy. He kept them waiting some time for their answer, and when they got it it was a flat refusal of all their demands.

The Hanseatic monopoly in England was a thing of the past, and the German merchants had to make the best of matters, and try what it was like to trade in an open field without any favour.

In Brussels and France, Krefting had slightly better success, and for the time being certain privileges were restored to the League, but it was very evident that there was no longer any hope of the League ever being restored to its old position.

In vain Krefting exercised all his ingenuity to set the League on its feet again ; he could not bring any unity into the Cities and all his diplomacy was wasted.

The League was still to figure during the troubled time of the Thirty Years' War, and even as late as the Napoleonic Campaigns, but it was to write no more glorious pages in the history of German commerce.

The League was no longer anything but a name and not even a name to conjure with : Elizabeth had administered the fatal blow and the Hansa was dead.

DOOR-KNOCKER

CHAPTER XIX

THE religious question, which had been such a vital factor in breaking down the unity of the League Cities, was now to plunge the whole of the German Empire into a prolonged period of war.

Although the Thirty Years' War itself lies outside the province of this book, it was instrumental in putting an end to all that remained of the Hanseatic League.

Prior to the opening of hostilities, various of the countries involved made overtures to the Hansa with a view to forming a defensive and offensive alliance with that once powerful body. The most persistent of these was Gustav Adolf of Sweden, who thought that his enmity with Denmark would influence the League in his favour. He did everything in his power to persuade the Hansa to agree to an alliance with Sweden, but with the passing years the League had grown distrustful of kingly promises, in addition to which they recognized their weakness and hoped, by declining to ally themselves with any of the participants, to profit by their neutrality during what they knew would be a protracted and disastrous struggle.

France sent her representatives to sue for an alliance ;

and, stranger still, a like proposition was made by their old enemy, Denmark; but to each and all they accorded a guarded refusal.

Finally they were approached by Spain, and that suit was strongly favoured by the Emperor Rudolph II, who hoped to gain some mercantile advantage from the use of the Spanish fleet; but the Hansa was wary, they remembered all the times when the Emperors had refused their requests, and in addition they felt a very deep distrust of Catholic Spain. Without giving a decided refusal, the heads of the League asked for time to consider the matter, and then set the whole proposition on one side. Later on the wisdom of this policy was clearly proved, when time brought to light the fact that the Emperor had ordered the general of his forces, Tilly, to seize various of the Hanseatic towns.

During the Thirty Years' War many of the Free Cities suffered terribly, and those who were fortunate enough to escape without being ravaged by either German or foreign troops had to expend vast sums of money in buying their immunity. The troubled times put an end to all trade prosperity and destroyed for ever the remaining remnants of the Hanseatic League.

It was in vain that the League tried to enforce the neutrality of its Free Cities. Stralsund suffered a long and bitter siege at the hands of Wallenstein, the general of the Catholic troops, and it was only due to the heroism and fortitude of the inhabitants that the town did not fall, for the dying League could offer it no kind of help or protection. Wismar, Wärnemunde,

Stade and Rostock fell into the hands of the troops, and were cruelly sacked, and this after they had paid large sums in their endeavours to maintain their neutrality.

Bremen suffered but little during the Thirty Years' War and was practically unaffected except by the prevailing sad state of affairs throughout the country. Hamburg also was fortunate, for in 1615 the city had begun to build new and extensive fortifications ; and it was to these fortifications that the city owed her immunity during the war ; for both Wallenstein and Tilly advanced upon Hamburg, but they evidently considered it too hard a task to tackle, for it was never besieged.

Naturally it suffered from the appalling conditions that prevailed throughout the country which was overrun by various armies, made up for the most part of lawless soldiers who ravaged wherever they passed and preyed upon friend and enemy alike. The city was overcrowded by refugees and suffered severely from plague and famine, added to which there were violent riots which resulted in much damage to private property.

Lübeck, placed as she was so near the field of Wallenstein's activities, was in the worst position. Great sums of money were expended on keeping a garrison for the protection of the harbour of Trävemunde, in addition to which large amounts went in buying her immunity from having troops quartered in the city. Meanwhile her outlying lands were overrun by the soldiers of both German generals, who left little prosperity behind them.

This state of affairs persisted long after the Peace of Münster brought to a conclusion the thirty disastrous years of war, for during the war between Sweden and Denmark, which followed, Lübeck had to continue her bribes in order to purchase a certain amount of favourable treatment for herself and her outlying lands.

The populace, annoyed at the greatly increased taxes, levied to make up the vast amounts required, rose in revolt, and did much wanton damage in the city; but this had one good result, for the Senate, alarmed at the demonstrations, made drastic changes in the governing body, which, under its new form, included members of the democratic party. But for all this Lübeck managed its intricate finances so well that the city was not entirely ruined.

The Thirty Years' War, which ended in 1648 with the Peace of Münster, left a Germany that was almost as lawless and unsafe as it had been in the early days of the Hanseatic League; and the Free Cities took many years to make good their losses both financial and commercial, and to re-establish their prosperous trade.

As a League of Cities the Hansa was no more, and at the last Diet, held in Lübeck in 1630, the few remaining affairs of the Hanseatic League had been put under the control of Bremen, Hamburg and Lübeck, which now entered into a close alliance that was to be the last shadowy survival of the great League.

There was all too little business to be done, but such as there was was left entirely in the hands of the three Cities; and it was Bremen, Hamburg and

Lübeck, as the last representatives of the Hanseatic League, who arranged for the sale of the two remaining Kontors at Antwerp and the Steelyard.

After the Diet of 1630, Lübeck still clung to a last faint hope of restoring the League to its old position ; but this soon proved utterly impossible, and all ideas of a reunited Hansa were abandoned.

During the Thirty Years' War, Bremen had suffered many vicissitudes ; it had been coveted and intrigued for by Denmark, and had fallen under the nominal suzerainty of Sweden after the Peace of Münster. After the city threw off the Swedish yoke, the Archbishopric of Bremen was sold to England, then under the rule of George I, the Elector of Hanover ; and, in 1730, George II recognized it as a Free City.

Even the Thirty Years' War was not to be the last of the troubles to afflict the remaining Hanseatic Towns. Their fate as Free Cities was to tremble in the balance more than once during the Napoleonic Wars, and again they were to suffer all the horrors of depleted coffers and the ruin caused by quartered troops.

Bremen was occupied by French troops and was incorporated in Napoleon's Empire, but it was given back its independence by the Congress of Vienna ; afterwards it joined, first, the North German Federation, and at a later date the Zollverein, or Customs Union of Germany, after which it was merged in the German Empire.

In 1783 Hamburg experienced a big increase in trade following on the Treaty of Paris which declared America an independent state. This was the be-

ginning of the close maritime connection between that
city and America. During the Napoleonic Wars,
Hamburg suffered severely. In 1807, Napoleon's
governor of the Hanseatic Cities, Bernadotte, entered
Hamburg with a demand for over fifteen million marks.
During the French occupation the city suffered
severely under the stern rule of Davoust, but worse
was to come. After the French defeat of 1812, the
Hansa Cities formed a Hanseatic Legion for the freeing
of their compatriots. Hamburg supplied four thousand
men and proceeded to give battle to Davoust, but they
were beaten and the city was retaken, and a more
severe régime than ever instituted. The banks were
sacked, and incredible amounts of money were taken
by the French, in addition to which much wanton
damage was done to property.

But 1814 saw the end of the French in Hamburg,
and the citizens started to restore their ruined commerce. After the Napoleonic Wars there was a great
trade revival and the industrious and clever Hamburg
merchants were soon marching on the road to prosperity.

It was with great reluctance that the Free Hanseatic
City of Hamburg finally joined the Zollverein in 1888.

It was not until 1917 that the last vestige of the old
Hanseatic League passed from Hamburg when a
commission was appointed by the *Bürgerschaft* (representative assembly of citizens) to reform the old Hanseatic Class franchise which had been the form of
government in Bremen, Hamburg and Lübeck. Under
the new régime the Senate became a democratic
parliamentary governing body, the power being in

the hands of the *Bürgerschaft*, the Senate not being
elected for life, as in the old days, but for a term of
years.

This reform applied equally to Bremen and Lübeck,
and with it passed the last vestige of the power of the
old Hanseatic Merchant government in the Free
Cities.

Lübeck, no longer the famous city that was the head
of the Hanseatic League throughout the years of its
greatness, was once more to have its peace disturbed
during the Napoleonic struggle ; and this time the
city was to experience such brutalities at the hands
of the French as had never been dreamed of, even in
those troubled times.

In 1803, Blücher, pursued by Bernadotte and Soult,
took refuge in Lübeck.   In vain did Blücher, with the
help of Generals Scharnhorst and Yorck, try to hold
the town against the French ; after some hours of
fierce fighting the city fell.

Then for three days Lübeck, once the pride of the
Hansa, was delivered over to the French troops, whose
brutality was beyond description.   Afterwards Bernadotte managed to restrain his men, but the occupation
of the city was disastrous.   All English imported
goods were seized by the French and destroyed ; in
addition, they condescended to accept enormous sums
of money.

This was the end of Lübeck as a rich and prosperous
trading city ; and even with the departure of the
French, after 1812, and the restoration of peace, only
a very modified trade returned to the City on the Träve.
It remains merely a town with a great historic past.

Yet Lübeck, peacefully dreaming in the shadow of its sea-green spires, still retains much of the ancient glory of the Hanseatic League; and through its crooked, winding streets, overshadowed by the old, crow-stepped buildings, steal the ghosts of those proud Hanseatic diplomats who led the League through its stirring history; and the rooms of the Rathus still seem to echo to the steps of Perseval, the Warrendorfs, Jacob and Johan Pleskow, Simon Swerting, Heinrich Westhoff, Wullenweber, David Gloxin and many another whose name has come down to us as having played his part in the stirring drama of the Hanseatic League.

KETTLE

CHAPTER XX

THE LAST YEARS OF THE STEELYARD

AFTER the closing of the Steelyard by Elizabeth in 1598, many of the German merchants still remained in England, while the League were carrying on their unsuccessful efforts to get back their property.

Although James refused to restore their ancient privileges, he finally gave the Steelyard back to the German merchants on condition that English merchants abroad were allowed to trade freely in the Hanseatic Cities. Certain of the German merchants took up their quarters at the Steelyard, but it was never more a Hanseatic Kontor in the accepted sense of the word.

But, despite the loss of all its former glory, the Steelyard had many years of more or less eventful history, and frequently figured in the Acts of Privy Council and the State Papers Domestic.

During their absence from the Steelyard the Hansa was greatly perturbed as to the upkeep of the building, and they addressed a pathetic and heartfelt appeal to the Lord Mayor, begging him to preserve the house with all care and above all not to allow coal to be stored in the garden.[1]

But, for all that, the building suffered greatly and

[1] Acts of Privy Council, Elizabeth. CCLIX . . . 49.

on their return the German merchants found it in a sorry condition. They promptly appealed to Lübeck for money with which to restore the Steelyard to some semblance of its former magnificence, but the affairs of the League were in no condition to allow of its sending money to England.

At this period there were but few Hanseats remaining in London, and only about eight men were resident in Thames Street. Yet despite the decline in the Hanseatic League, the English still envied the German merchants their trade, and in 1610 James gave orders for the seizure of all Hansa ships found upon the high seas. Gone indeed was the ancient power of the Hansa, when it could do nothing stronger than voice its resentment at this further insult !

With the accession of Charles I a certain amount of favour and protection was accorded to the remaining Hanseats of the Steelyard, but in spite of this there were constant attempts to wrest the Thames Street buildings from the Germans.

It was at this time that the League sent two prominent Hamburg men to take over the control of their London affairs, and it was largely due to the energy and diplomacy of Möller and van Aitzema that Charles still upheld the Germans against the attacks of the English, and allowed them to retain the Steelyard and their other depots at Lynn and Boston.

Although the business passing through the Steelyard was in no way comparable with that of the old days of the Hanseatic monopoly, there was still a considerable profit accruing to the League from the English trade, and the expenses were few, now that no state was kept up in the Kontor. The English constantly complained that the Steelyard was no longer a storehouse for merchandise or a trading depot, but that the Germans merely let out the various buildings and enjoyed a good rent from them.

In 1647 the Kontor-mastership was given to Jacob Jacobsen, a man who was to figure largely in the later history of the Steelyard. It was solely due to his loyal and unselfish policy that the last remnants of the League were able to sell the buildings in 1853. He was an honest and straightforward man, and the heads of the League in Lübeck treated him very badly.

On Sunday, September 3rd, 1666, the main portion of the Thames Street building was destroyed by the Great Fire of London, and Jacobsen only just managed to escape with his life. After the Fire of London the City Authorities stated that they intended to confiscate all sites which had not been rebuilt upon within a stated period.

Jacobsen sent word of the disaster to Lübeck, and urged the immediate forwarding of the necessary money with which to rebuild the Steelyard before the expiration of the period of grace. Hamburg, Bremen and Lübeck, as the last representatives of the League, called a meeting in Hamburg in 1669, but few towns attended, and those that did were obstinate in their refusal to furnish any portion of the money.

On hearing that no money was forthcoming from Lübeck, Jacobsen obtained an extension from the Civic authorities, and once more made every endeavour to get the required funds from the League, pointing out how fatal it would be to allow the valuable property to lapse into the hands of the English. But it was all in vain, and finally, in despair of ever obtaining money from the League, Jacobsen decided to rebuild, at least the main portion—that facing Thames Street, at his own expense.

He came to an arrangement with one John Ball, to erect a building on the site of the old guildhall with a frontage upon Thames Street, and six houses and an archway opening into Windgoose Lane.

The arms of the League, carved in stone, were placed above the main gate, and the following record of the transaction appeared in the account books of the Steelyard :

" On Dec 31st., 1670, to Gabriel Cibbert,
    stonecutter, for the eagles to put on
    over the gate of John Ball's building £5."

The Latin inscription runs : Si-Mercat-Hanse-Theutoni-Lond-in-Regno-ang-residen.

This stone, now preserved at the Guildhall, had a strange history. For many years it was lost, and was finally found by Mr. Lawrence Weaver, in the garden of Bickley Hall.

Other amusing items in the account books were :

" 1656. To the Klinke across the water,
    yearly according to custom .   .   £-.10.4.
To scavenger, his weekly dole, besides
    what he carries away .   .   .   £4.
1662. To the dogs keeper, for the up-
    keep of the dogs their collars etc. £3.5. –
To the gardener for cutting the vines. £1.5. –
Spent with Dr. Skinner and others at
    Whitehall, Westminster, the Temple
    and in taverns .   .   .   . £12.18.– "

Even after Jacobsen had saved the Steelyard by using his own money for rebuilding it the heads of the League refused to pay him back. After his death, his brother, Theodore, was made Kontor-master, and for many years the Court of Chancery was considering the case of Jacobsen *v.* Hansa, till in 1748 they gave their decision and the Hansa were ordered to pay £3,000 to the Jacobsen family.

Both the Jacobsens were prominent members of the congregation and were instrumental in the re-fitting of the new church that was built after the Great Fire. They never severed their connection with All Hallows, although both Jacob and Theodore, together with other German merchants resident in London, were granted Letters Patent in 1670, for the erection of a Lutheran church in Trinity Lane. They gave various sums of money towards the restoration of the church and presented it with several beautiful fitments.

One of the outstanding features of the church was the finely carved wooden screen with the Hanseatic Eagles in its centre panel. Various authorities have declared it to be the work of a Hamburg carver, and stated that it was presented to All Hallows the More by the Hanseatic League ; but much doubt has been cast on both these statements, and the screen is now acknowledged to be a fine example of English wood-carving of the period ; and as having been the gift of Theodore Jacobsen alone.

It is very unlikely that the League, which could not even provide funds for the rebuilding of the Steelyard, should present anything to the church. The Jacob-sens were certainly men of considerable wealth, or

Jacob could never have afforded to erect the Thames Street building at his own expense, and they had always evinced a lively interest in the church.

Theodore Jacobsen also presented a carved pulpit and sounding-board, a lectern and clerk's pew.

Upon the death of Jacob Jacobsen his brother had him buried in the unfinished church of All Hallows the More and, at a later date, placed a stone to his memory on the wall, bearing the following inscription :

" Sacred to the memory of Jacob Jacobsen, who with the support of the illustrious Council of the Hanseatic Towns of Germany, was a most worthy master and president for thirty-three years, of the Guildhall or house of the same situated here in the Steelyard. Which after the destructive Fire of London, he, as a munificent restorer had rebuilt from the ashes with even greater splendour than before."

In spite of the newly-built Lutheran church the remaining members of the Steelyard still continued to worship at All Hallows the More, where certain pews were reserved for Hanseats until 1894, when the church was pulled down.

With the dismantling of the church the memorial stone to Jacob Jacobsen was set up in St. Michael, Paternoster Royal, and the screen, pulpit and sounding-board in St. Margaret's, Lothbury ; but, at a later date, by some grave mismanagement, the sounding-board and pulpit were separated, the latter being banished to a church in Hammersmith.[1]

[1] Authority for the material concerning All Hallows the More : " Notes on the Latter History of the Steelyard in London," by Philip Norman, LL.D., pp. 389-426. *Archæologia*, Vol. 61, Part 2, 1909.

It seems a great pity that this fine pulpit and sounding-board cannot once more be united, to remain as a memorial to Kontor-master Theodore Jacobsen in the form in which he presented them to the famous old Hanseatic church of All Hallows the More.

The last conecting link between the Hanseatic League and London was severed in 1853, when, after long negotiations, Hamburg, Bremen and Lübeck sold the Steelyard buildings to Mr. Morrison and Mr. John Pemberton Heyward for the sum of £72,500. The site is now occupied by Cannon Street Railway Station.

FIRE-PUMP

CHAPTER XXI

CONCLUSION

THE once mighty Hanseatic League had passed from a world whose changed conditions rendered its methods obsolete and impracticable.

Various causes, political, social, economic and geographical, contributed to its downfall ; but by far the most important factor in its decline was the tenacity with which its leaders adhered to an autocratic and short-sighted insistence on total monopoly, and their obstinate refusal to grant equal rights to their foreign rivals in the field of commerce.

At an early date the end of the League was foreshadowed by the union of various countries—that of Poland and Lithuania in 1386, of the Scandinavian countries, under the Union of Kalmar, in 1395, which, although this union was broken at a later date, severely crippled the Hanseatic trade in the Baltic ; and in 1466 when, by the Treaty of Thorn, the whole of West Prussia was ceded to Poland, with the resultant loss to the Hansa of the powerful Vistula Cities.

The migration of the herrings, which began about 1425, led to a further falling off in the Baltic trade and to the rapid rise to commercial and mercantile supremacy of the Dutch, and involved Lübeck in a series of disastrous wars with the Scandinavians and the Hollanders.

About this time, too, the English began to wake to
the realization of the latent possibilities of their own
trade, and as soon as they turned their serious attention
to commerce the Hanseats found themselves faced
with powerful rivals, equipped with large and sea-
worthy ships, who threatened their cherished monopolies in all their most profitable trading centres.   In
addition to this, the discovery of the new world opened
up fresh markets and the main stream of trade was
deflected from Germany, while the ports on the
Atlantic took the place of those on the Mediterranean.

From being excellently placed on the main routes
of the whole trade across Europe, the Hanseatic Cities
now found themselves in an isolated position with
regard to this new trade ; also, and this was an important point, the Germans were no longer essential
as middlemen and carriers, and it was on this basis
alone that the Hanseatic League had risen to power.

With these great changes in the times the League
found itself with a government that was totally in-
adequate to cope with the new crises that arose.
Always a loose and amorphous body, the League had
never created a solid and fixed governing organization.
The affairs of the Cities had been managed by Lübeck,
with the help of a majority vote of the City Representatives on all questions of policy ; but as the years
passed, and the Free Cities increased in size and
wealth, many of them grew jealous of Lübeck as the
head of the Hansa and showed a strong reluctance to
abide by its rulings.   Frequently questions arose that
did not affect the League as a whole, and often in later
years Lübeck was drawn into disagreements, quarrels

and wars in which the other League cities refused to take any part ; in fact, there was a growing lack of unity among the League Cities that shook the Hansa to its very foundations.

During the period of its greatness the heads of the Hanseatic League had been able to control the Cities ; the final punishment of boycott and un-Hansing led to poverty and ruin, and was a strong weapon for the maintenance of order ; but with the growing increase of foreign trade a city could be sure of maintaining its position and even of increasing in prosperity, by defying the Hansa and opening its gates to the foreign merchants ; thus the League's threat of un-Hansing no longer held any terror for the disaffected Cities.

Gone were the days when the whole of the trade of Northern Europe passed through the hands of the League and when its boycott of a City or Nation was the prelude to disaster.

The Hanseatic League had been brought into being by a body of rich merchants with the sole idea of making money. It was not backed by any manufacturing or agricultural interest, and throughout its history the leaders sternly repressed the democratic classes in the cities and ruthlessly excluded them from any participation in the government, with the result that with the evolution of the proletariat the League found this ever more powerful party arrayed against them. The Hansa was a body of men without the slightest vestige of altruism and like all egoistic and inelastic organizations the day came when its own policy led it to its downfall.

Another reason for this downfall lay in the fact that

the League stood alone ; all through its history the Hansa had insisted upon its neutrality, and in the early days it had certainly reaped a rich reward for its services to the various warring parties ; but, with the growth of union and strong government among many of the nations, and the slow but steady decay in the Holy Roman Empire, the League were to suffer from the lack of any strong government behind them. Added to this the League Cities were scattered over a wide area and were isolated among territories that owed their allegiance to various overlords, all at enmity one with the other ; thus it became utterly impossible to maintain the close union necessary to weld the League into one solid body.

But in spite of all these difficulties the Hanseatic League might have kept its position as a powerful body of Cities, united in their trade interests, if the heads of the organization had moved with the times and adapted their policy to the changed conditions. Unfortunately there was no such tradition behind the League. It had risen to power on a policy of strict monopoly, which in the early years it had been able to maintain by either forcing, or bribing, foreign monarchs to grant special privileges to Hanseatic Merchants. Now those years were gone, never to return, and with them was gone all hope of the Hanseatic monopoly ; yet the heads of the League were incapable of realizing this and persisted in demanding the impossible. In the latter days of the League no leader arose who was strong enough, or, for the matter of that, far-sighted enough, to institute a change in policy and insist on the Hanseats taking their place as the equals of all the other merchants in the rich new world of commerce.

So the Hanseatic League disintegrated. Just as its birth was slow and protracted, its death crept on almost imperceptibly, with long pauses during which matters were at a standstill : but eventually the end arrived, and with the sale of the Antwerp Kontor in 1863 the League passed for ever.

In its hey-day the Hansa had been a powerful and mighty organization whose financial power had enabled them to dictate terms to kings and emperors. It had been responsible for the spread of trade and prosperity, and for the establishment of civic power, throughout the cities of Northern Europe ; conceived in a rough and brutal age, the League had spread culture and civilization throughout its far-flung realm, and its name will ever remain in history gloriously associated with the first Free Cities of Europe.

One is tempted to wonder if the new German Luft Hansa will ever write as glorious a chapter in the commercial history of the air as those gallant, unscrupulous, old Hanseatic merchants wrote on sea and land.

THE BERGEN LION

BIBLIOGRAPHY

Hansisches Urkundenbuch. K. Kunze and W. Stein. (10 vols., Halle and Leipzig, 1876–1907.)

Inventare hansischer Archive des sechzehnten Jahrhunderts. (2 vols., 1896–1903.)

Hansische Geschichtblätter. (14 vols., 1871–1908.)

Geschichte des hanseatischen Bundes. G. F. Sartorius. (3 vols., Göttingen, 1802–1808.)

Urkundliche Geschichte des Ursprunges der deutschen Hanse. J. M. Lappenberg. (2 vols., Hamburg, 1830.)

Die Hansestädte und König Waldemar von Dänemark. D. Schäfer. (Jena, 1879.)

Beiträge zur Geschichte der deutschen Hanse. W. Stein. (Giessen, 1900.)

Urkundliche Geschichte des hansischen Stahlhofes zu London. (J. M. Lappenberg, Hamburg, 1851.)

Die deutsche Hanse. T. Lindner. (Leipzig, 1911.)

Die Blütezeit der deutschen Hanse. E. Daenell. (2 vols., Berlin, 1905–6.)

Die deutsche Hanse. D. Schäfer. (Bielefeld and Leipzig, 1914.)

Hamburg und England im Zeitalter der Königin Elisabeth. R. Ehrenberg. Jena, 1896.)

Histoire Commerciale de la Ligue Hanséatique. Emile Worms. (Paris, 1864.)

Die deutsche Hansa in Russland. A. Winckler. (Berlin, 1886.)

Der Stapelzwang des Hansischen Kontors zu Brügge im fünfzehnten Jahrhundert. H. Rogge. (Kiel, 1903.)

GERMANY	SCANDINAVIA	RUSSIA
		11th Century. German Merchants in Russia.
1157 Treaty between Henry II and Frederick Barbarossa.		
	1227 Hansa defeated the Danes at Bornhoved.	
1241 Hamburg and Lübeck Protective Alliance.	1229 Gotland Hansa treaty with Russia secured privileges for Novgorod Kontor. Same year Gotland Hansa signed a similar treaty with England.	1229 Gotland Hansa acquired privileges in Novgorod.
	1249 Lübeck won naval victory over Eric II.	
		1346 Lombards excluded from Novgorod.
1359 First Diet held at Lübeck.		1350 Mention of "Theutonicorum Hansa."
1367 Diet at Cologne decides on war with Valdemar.	1361 Sack of Visby by Valdemar Atterdag.	1361 Hanseatic embassage to Novgorod to enforce "Lübeck Law."
1370 Treaty of Stralsund.	1370 Treaty of Stralsund.	
1374 Brunswick un-Hansed.		
1375 Emperor Charles visits Lübeck.		
1385 Union of Poland and Lithuania.	1393 Bergen sacked by Victual Brother Pirates.	
	1395 Union of Kalmar.	
1405 Edict against the Lombards.	1402 Stortebecker captured.	
1418 Lübeck recognized as head of the League.	1425 Herrings began to leave the Baltic.	
1447 Largest Diet held at Lübeck—36 Cities.	1428 Bartel Bot sacked Bergen.	
1466 Treaty of Thorn. Vistula Cities leave the League.		
1471-6 Cologne un-Hansed.		1473 Ivan III's attack on Kontor at Novgorod.
		1478 Hanseats expelled from Novgorod.

CHART

THE LOW COUNTRIES	ENGLAND	KINGS OF ENGLAND
		1066–1087 William I.
		1087–1100 William II.
		1100–1135 Henry I.
		1135–1154 Stephen.
		1154–1189 Henry II.
	1157 Treaty between Henry II and Barbarossa.	
	1194 Richard I's charter to Cologne merchants.	1189–1199 Richard I.
	1199 John confirmed German privileges.	1199–1216 John.
		1216–1272 Henry III
	1229 Gotland Hansa obtained privileges in England.	
1252 Privileges granted to German merchants.		
1260 Gotland Hansa acquired privileges in Flanders which led to the foundation of the Kontor at Bruges.	1303 Carta Mercatoria.	1272–1307 Edward I. 1307–1327 Edward II. 1327–1377 Edward III
1347 Statutes of German merchants in Bruges.		
1358 Embargo on trade with Flanders.		
1360 Full Hanseatic privileges restored in Bruges.		
	1377 Richard II confirmed Hanseatic privileges.	1377–1399 Richard II.
		1399–1413 Henry IV
	1412 Scotland un-Hansed.	
		1413–1422 Henry V
	1422 First mention of the Steelyard.	1422–1461 Henry VI.
1425 Herrings began to spawn in the North Sea.		
1451 Hansa left Bruges for six years.	1447 Henry VI suspended Hanseatic privileges.	
		1461–1483 Edward IV
1474 Treaty of Utrecht.	1474 Treaty of Utrecht. Edward IV renewed Hanseatic privileges.	1483–1485 Richard III. 1485–1509 Henry VII.
1488 Bruges under the displeasure of Emperor Frederick III.	1490 Henry VII forbade export of wool in German bottoms.	

CHRONOLOGICAL

GERMANY	SCANDINAVIA	RUSSIA
		1494 End of Kontor.
	1510 Hansa captured Born-holm.	
	1519 Gustav Vasa escaped to Lübeck.	
1531 Lübeck adopts Luther-anism.		
1549 Merchant Adventurers remove from Antwerp to Hamburg.		1553 English first made their way to Moscow via Archangel.
	1560 Sweden freed from the domination of the Hansa.	
1570 Emperor Maximilian presided over Diet at Frankfurt.	1576 Bornholm ceded to the Danes.	
1597 Emperor's edict order-ing all English mer-chants to leave Ger-man soil.	1591 Last of the Bergen Initiations.	1586 Privileges granted to Hansa in Narva and Pleskov.
1603 Hansa embassage to Muscovite Court.		
1618 Commencement of Thirty Years War.		
1630 Last Diet held at Lübeck. Authority vested in Bremen, Hamburg and Lübeck.		
1648 Peace of Westphalia ends Thirty Years War		
	1775 Bergen Kontor sold.	
1783 Growth of Hamburg's trade with America.		
1806 Lübeck sacked by the French.		
1807 Bernadotte appointed Governor of the Han-seatic Cities.		
1811 Davoust entered Ham-burg.		
1814-15 Congress at Vienna. Bremen, Hamburg and Lübeck declared Free Cities.		
1869 Lübeck joined the Zoll-verein.		
1888 Bremen and Hamburg joined the Zollverein.		
1917 Old Hanseatic form of Government in Bre-men, Hamburg and Lübeck abolished.		

CHART (*continued*)

THE LOW COUNTRIES	ENGLAND	KINGS OF ENGLAND
1494 Fall of the Bruges Kontor.		
1510 (about) Low Countries hold most of the carrying trade.		1509–1547 Henry VIII.
1545 Decision to move Kontor to Antwerp.		
		1547–1553 Edward VI.
	1553 English opened up White Sea route to Russia.	1553–1558 Mary.
	1560 Hansa embassage to Elizabeth.	1558–1603 Elizabeth.
1568 Hall of the Easterlings in Antwerp completed.	1567 Merchant Venturers Treaty with Hamburg.	
	1597 Edict against English merchants in Germany.	
	1598 Hanseats left the Steelyard by the order of Elizabeth.	
	1604 Embassage under Krefting of Bremen to James I to ask for a renewal of privileges failed.	1603–1625 James I.
	1611 Steelyard restored to Hansa.	
1624 Antwerp Kontor taken over by Spaniards.		1625–1649 Charles I.
		1649–1661 Cromwell.
	1666 Most of Steelyard buildings burnt in the Great Fire of London.	1661–1685 Charles II.
		1685–1689 James II.
		1689–1702 William and Mary.
		1702–1714 Anne.
		1714–1727 George I.
		1727–1760 George II.
		1760–1820 George III.
		1820–1830 George IV.
		1830–1837 William IV
		1837–1901 Victoria.
1863 Antwerp Kontor building sold.	1853 Steelyard sold by Bremen, Hamburg and Lübeck.	
		1901–1910 Edward VII.
		1910– George V.

INDEX

AA, Sir John de, 82
Abbehale, Ralph de, 181
Abel, Richard, 84
Åbo, 103
Adam of Bremen, 53
Adams, Thomas, 85, 86
Agincourt, Battle of, 22
Aitzema, —, van, 251
Albert of Sweden, 78, 103
All Hallows the More, Church of, 176, 254, 255, 256
Almaine, Merchants of, 143 *sqq.*, 152, 170
Almayne (*see also* Germany), 43
Alps, the, 35
Alterderne, Ralph de, 181
Alwey, Robert, 88
America, 246, 247
Amsterdam, 74, 204
Amsterdam Sea Law, 61, 204
Anold, 85
Antarctic Star, the, 42, 43
Antwerp, 16, 204–5, 206, 207, 210, 213, 217, 218, 234, 246, 261
    Hall of the Easterlings at, 205, 206, 210
ap Fen, Hugh, 86
Archangel, 129, 188, 199, 220, 225
Arkez, 47
Atlantic Ports, 258
Augsburg, 8, 13, 16, 34, 136

BAATU, 46
Ball, John, 253

Baltic Cities, 68, federation of, 8, 11
Baltic Sea, coasts and trade (*see also* Herring Fishery, Pirates, *and* Victual Brothers), 6, 16 *sqq.*, 23, 24, 35, 43, 57, 70, 164, 187, 188, 189, 191 *sqq.*, 195, 196, 200, 203, 204, 257
Bamme, Lord Mayor Adam, 20
Bardi, the, Bankers, 155
Barnacles (Bernakes), 48, 49
Barret, Alan, 89
Bartholomew, Friar, of Cremona, 45
Bartke-Snyder, 22
Bartram of Hamburdge, 168
Basle, 34
Beauchamp, John de, Admiral of the South, 180
Belyetere, Edmund, 90
Bergen, 16, 34, 37, 79, 81, 90, 100, 104 *sqq.*, 124, 125, 127, 130, 131, 152, 154, 160, 162, 165, 175, 176, 187, 189, 210
    " Bridge of the Lice " at, 106
    " Gardens " at, 108 *sqq.*
    Initiations at, 109, 111 *sqq.*
    Maria Kirche of, 115–16
Bernadotte, 247, 248
Bets, William, 87
Bevis, John, 156
Beytonuse Bay, 27
Bibliography, 263
Bickley Hall, 253

269